Contents

C000177928

Reading Skills

Writing Skills

Hot Tips

Look out for our expert exam advice designed to help you improve your revision and exam techniques.

Start Strong - Finish Strong

Your guide

- The more you engage with this guide, the more you will get out of it.
- Complete your own responses to both the reading and writing questions before looking at those provided.
- After that, compare answers, and grade them using your particular exam board's mark scheme to see where you could have picked up more marks.
- Listen to the audio content of this guide on a regular basis to internalise it.
- Have a go at providing your own examples for the literary techniques shown in the Reading Section.

Your revision

- Firstly, look back at everything you've done in class and for homework over the course of your GCSE English Language studies, to revise what you've done, and to identify any areas that need further work.
- Look at past papers in order to familiarise yourself with the number of questions, question style and marks on offer. Knowing what to expect will help you to feel more relaxed about the examination process.
- Complete past papers, the more you do, the better you'll become.
- Build up to completing a past paper under timed conditions. The first time you attempt one, don't set yourself any time limit, just work through the questions to the best of your ability. After that, start to limit your time, until you are able to complete a paper under exam conditions.
- Use past paper mark schemes to grade your own work and set yourself targets for improvement.
- Work out timings so you know how long you can spend on each question when it comes to the exam.
- If you are entitled to an amanuensis in the exam, ensure that you feel comfortable giving dictation.
- Read different text types in order to become familiar with their form, language and structure.
- Follow the news, especially current affairs that affect young adults, as this could provide valuable inspiration for your writing tasks.
- Play word games and browse round thesaurus websites in order to increase your vocabulary.

Your exam

- Read the questions carefully and respond to what they are asking you.
- Read the instructions carefully so that you do the specified amount of questions, without missing any out or completing extra, unnecessary questions.
- When you do the longer questions, it's worth spending a short amount of time devising a plan in order to complete a coherent and comprehensive answer.
- As you read through the stexts for the Reading Section, highlight and jot down brief notes about anything that strikes you as useful, this will help you to find it again once you come to write your answers.
- It is essential to leave enough time at the end of the exam in order to check through your work. This is a key strategy for picking up technical errors such as spelling mistakes or missing punctuation.

Sensory Language

Sensory language enables readers to connect with a piece of writing on a very immediate, physical level.

Alliteration

- Alliteration is when the **same consonant sound** is used in quick succession.
- Alliteration is a powerful technique that produces a **pleasing sound** within a piece of writing, it also has the effect of making writing **memorable**, so it is used for key points.
'I find fickle friends frustrating.'

Sibilance

- Sibilance is a **particular type of alliteration** where fricatives such as 's' or 'sh' are the repeated sound.
- Sibilance produces a **sustained hissing** sound within a piece of writing and can be used to convey **sighs**, **whispers** or even a **sense of threat**.
'The wasp swarm was suffocated into silence by the smoky air.'

Onomatopoeia

- Onomatopoeia is when the sound of the word has a **direct connection** to the sound that it describes.
- Onomatopoeia makes a piece of writing **dynamic** because it has a distinct, **sensory effect** upon the reader.
'As he stepped on stage, his heart pounded, beat after beat after beat.'

Appeal to the senses

- Writers like to appeal to their reader's senses using figurative and sensory language.
- Appealing to the senses helps to make a piece of writing accessible because the writer is sharing common feelings to do with sight, sound, touch, taste and smell.
- In a piece of writing, consider the finer points of the 5 senses:

Sight - colour, distance, focus, light, movement, peripheral vision.
Sound - direction, distance, music, pitch, rhyme, rhythm, speech, volume.
Touch - balance, humidity, pain, pressure, temperature.
Taste - flavour, texture.
Smell - decay, familiar, fragrant, pungent, sharp, soft, unfamiliar.

Figurative Language

Figurative language will elevate and enrich a piece of writing, help to direct the reader's attention to key ideas, as well as keeping them entertained.

Similes

- A simile is when a **comparison** is made using '**as**' or '**like**' to make a direct connection.
- The comparison element is both an efficient and elegant way of providing the reader with clarity and extra information about a point.
  'I was always terrible with money, it just ran through my hands like water through sand.'

Metaphors

- A metaphor is when an **indirect comparison** is made by **juxtaposing two elements**.
- The comparison element allows a writer to give their readers vivacious and innovative perspectives.
  'I am an island, surrounded by a sea of grief.'

Extended Metaphors

- If a writer **refers back** to an initial metaphor and **elaborates upon** it, they can create an extended metaphor.
- Extended metaphors allow writers to spotlight a key argument or idea, so that it is easier for the reader to follow.

Personification

- Personification is when a writer applies **human qualities** to something that is other than human.
- Using personification allows writers to provide their readers with added depth of meaning and emotion.
  'The weather was a cruel master and used his icy wind and rain to make us stay indoors.'

Hyperbole

- Hyperbole is when a writer **over exaggerates** an idea to make it stand out.
- This over exaggeration intensifies the power of the writing and can also be used to create comic effect.
  'It took an eternity to get served, I thought I'd die an old woman before the waitress noticed me.'

Litotes

- Litotes is when a writer **under exaggerates** an idea to make it stand out.
- The use of litotes can bring irony, emphasis and humour to a piece of writing.
  'Becoming the under 16 national champion for javelin is not a bad day's work.'

 Revise smarter: use the audio guide while you are doing your paper round/walking to school.

Figurative Language

Oxymoron

- An oxymoron is when two **opposing words or phases** are placed **side by side**.
- The apparently impossible image that an oxymoron conjures is used by writers in order to communicate multi-layered ideas, as well as often being employed to create humour. 'silent scream', 'working holiday', 'seriously funny'.

Paradox

- A paradox presents two ideas side by side, where the ideas are so different, they **can't possibly both exist at the same time**.
- Writers may use paradoxical statements in order to make their readers think or question the matter in hand.
  'The wisest person knows that they have not yet learned a thing.'

Ambiguity

- Ambiguity is created when a word or phrase has **two or more meanings** and it is unclear whether just one, or all meanings are intended.
- Ambiguity is used by writers in order to make readers explore different perspectives and think about what is being communicated.
  'I saw the woman using the telescope.'

Denotation

- Denotation is the **literal meaning** of a word or phrase.
- Writing may denote straightforward facts or figures.
  'The shop is open 24/7.'

Connotation

- Connotation is the **implied meaning** of a word or phrase.
- Writers use connotation in order to create depth in their work and communicate multi-layered meanings.
  'Look at her Prada handbag!' Brings connotations of admiration <u>and</u> jealousy.

Inference

- Inference is when a reader uses the information given to them by the writer, identifies the clues contained within the writing, clues provided by such elements as the connotations, in order to read between the lines, and draw a conclusion about what the writer is really saying.

Take a 5 minute break after each 50 minutes of revising. You can only take in so much information in one go!

Rhetoric

Rhetorical language is useful when writing to persuade, but it can also be used in creative writing, for example to add power to a particular character's speech.

4

Rhetorical questions

- A rhetorical question doesn't require a literal answer, it's designed to **provoke** an **emotional reaction** from the reader.
- Rhetorical questions can bring structure to a text as after asking one, the writer can go on to provide a response.
  'How would you feel if you came under suspicion because of your religion?'

Numerical Data

- Writers use numerical values such as percentages to support their writing.
- This create the effect that the writing is based on research and evidence, and therefore adds a sense of **credibility**.
  '98% of pupils said they'd preferred to have a healthy option at lunchtime.'

Counter arguments

- A counter argument is when a writer **anticipates** an opposing point of view and then shows why it is incorrect.
- Counter arguments will help to leave the reader feeling that they have to agree with the writer's point of view.
  'Some people will argue that renewable energy sources cannot replace the use of fossil fuels, however, this is untrue. Clearly, there needs to be investment and expansion in the renewable energy infrastructure but it is possible to develop this.'

Direct Appeal to the Reader and Parenthesis

- Writers often make a direct appeal to their readers by using **personal pronouns** such as 'us' and 'we'.
- This infers that there is a **bond** between the writer and the reader, making the readers feel an affinity towards the writer and therefore their point of view.
  'If we all work together, we can achieve a positive school environment.'
- Direct appeals can also be made using parenthetical phrases.
  'Preparing for GCSEs, I'm sure you'll admit, is a demanding process.'

Repetition is a key feature of rhetorical language and appears in many forms, it is used to emphasise key points.

Anadiplosis

- When a word or phrase is used at the end of a clause and then repeated at the beginning of the next clause.
  'When I call for help, I call for help from each and every one of you.'

Epistrophe

- When a word or phrase is repeated at the end of successive clauses.
  'When you're at work, you deserve respect, when you're at school you deserve respect, when you're at home, you deserve respect.'

Page 8

Anecdotes, Analogies and Allusions

Anecdotes

- An anecdote is a **short tale**, usually based on **personal experience**.
- Anecdotes can help a writer to strengthen an argument because it's a way of providing '**proof**' by giving an example.
- Anecdotes can also be **amusing** and therefore can add entertainment value to a piece of writing.
  'I myself have been in exactly this situation, as the other day, when I was walking my dog, Bertie ran off, and when I found him, he was covered in mud, sitting in the middle of a puddle.'

Analogies

- An analogy is when a **familiar concept** is used to illustrate a more complex or **unfamiliar idea**.
- Analogies allow writers to **clarify difficult ideas** in order to help their readers follow what they are writing about.
  'It can be useful to think of short-term memory like a post-it note, as both are used to store ideas that are in the process of being worked upon.'

Allusion

- Allusion is when a writer makes a reference to a person, place, object, literary work, myth, religious text, or historical event, (amongst other things).
- An allusion is like a **literary shortcut**, by making the reference, the writer is guiding their reader's thoughts to a bigger field of information, without having to explain it all within their own writing.
  'I've only told you to fetch me a library book, it's not like you've been asked to retrieve the Golden Fleece.'

Always read each question at least twice: misreading exam questions is far more common than you might think.

Humour

Writers often use humour in order to add entertainment value and depth to their writing.

Puns

- Puns make use of **homophones** and **homonyms** in order to offer multiple meanings or a play on words.
- Puns elevate a writer's work by adding both humour and layers of meaning.
  'My friend tried to annoy me with bird puns, but I retaliated...
  toucan play at that game.'

Tautology

- A tautology is when the **same point is made twice in succession**, rendering the second point unnecessary.
- If used deliberately, tautologies can create comedy and illustrate an absurd situation.
  'It was reported that the armed gunman was armed with a gun.'

Irony

- Irony is when the **implied meaning** of the language is the **inverse of the literal meaning**. This difference can be detected through the context and tone.
- Irony can be used to communicate negative feelings whilst simultaneous creating humour and this can make a reader more sympathetic to the writer's predicament or point of view.
  'It's great that Mr Manley won't give me an extension on the homework deadline.'

Caricature

- A caricature is when a character is presented in a way that **exaggerates** certain elements of their appearance or personality, while at the same time, ignoring their finer points, leading to a **grotesquely humorous** portrayal, rather than something more subtle or rounded.
- Caricatures are often found in parody and satire.

Parody

- A parody is a **deliberate imitation** of an existing work, where key elements of the original are **exaggerated**, usually for comic effect.
- Parodies can range from being a **fond tribute**, to a **mocking critique**.

Satire

- Satire is when a writer uses techniques such as irony, caricature and parody in order to **expose a perceived weakness**.
- Current affairs and political figures are often the subject matter of satire.

Tone and Register

Tone

- A writer's use of tone is how they **convey their attitude and feelings** in order to create a **mood**.
- This mood then engages the reader's emotions.
- For example, if a writer conveys a mood of apprehension, their reader is likely to feel sympathy in response.
  'I felt nervous and began to worry about what my new classmates would be like.'
- Tone is conveyed through structure, punctuation and language.
- For example, a succession of simple sentences, punctuated with an exclamation mark and using vocabulary pertaining to apathy, could create a tone of irritation.
  'I'm tired of this nonsense! I've seen it all before. I don't even want to look.'

Register

- Register is created through the **level of formality** used in a piece of writing.
- Writers will **vary their register according to their audience and purpose**.
- If there is a **distance** between the writer and their audience in terms of factors such as: age, friendship or status, it is likely that a **formal register** would be appropriate.
- However, if a writer is **close** to their audience in terms of the factors mentioned above, it's likely they would use an **informal register**.
- Formal language is created by using **Standard English** and is usually characterised by a **respectful tone**.
- Informal language can deviate from Standard English through the use of **slang**, **idioms** and **dialect**.
- In your exam you should aim to use Standard English for the majority of your writing and if you do deviate, it must be consciously crafted, in order to create a particular, controlled effect.
- For example, slang and dialect can be used to create a specific effect when voicing direct speech of characters, or within your own, or your narrator's voice. This can make your writing livelier for your reader.
- Using **jargon** and subject specific language can also affect the register of your writing, as this will enable you to convey a sense of authority.

Look back at your mock exam papers. What errors did you make? Do you know what you need to do to make sure that you don't repeat the same mistakes?

Word Classes and Their Uses

Being able to identify word classes and comment on their uses is one way to achieve a focused response to the high mark reading questions.

Nouns

- Nouns are naming words, used to refer to a person, place or object.
- Fiction writers are **careful when choosing nouns** for their characters, settings or significant objects, as these names add a **layer of meaning** into the text.
- For example, in a ghost story, the setting may have a name connected with death in order to help add to an atmosphere of dread and fear.

Adjectives

- Adjectives are describing words used to add detail about a character, setting or object.
- Writers apply **precisely chosen** adjectives to their characters, settings or significant objects in order to communicate **essential details** to the reader. This in turn shapes the reader's response to the text.
- For example, a writer could describe a boat as looking 'skeletal' in order to convey the fact that it is in a state of decay, and missing outer parts so that the underlying frame has become visible.
- Sometimes a writer will use a **group of adjectives** that all connect, for example, they might refer to the 'skeletal boat' as having 'ribs' and being 'bone white'.
- Such groupings create a **lexical field,** which adds depth and structure to a text.

Verbs

- Verbs are **action words**.
- Again, writers will be **precise** in their choice of verbs in order to achieve a particular effect.
- The use of verbs has a big impact on the **energy conveyed by a text**.
- For example, if a writer describes a boat as 'drifting' on water that is 'rippling' these quiet, gentle actions create a feeling of calm and tranquillity in the text.
- Writers can use a group of verbs that are all linked by meaning in order to create a lexical field.

Narrators, Eye-witnesses and Speakers

First Person Narrators

- A first person narrator is a character who is **present within a text**. They report their feelings and experiences.
- The first person narrator is usually the main character, however, supporting characters can also be used for first person narration.
- Be vigilant as writers can **use more than one first person narrator** within a text in order to give **multiple viewpoints**.
- First person narration can give the reader a **great insight** into the emotions and thoughts of a particular character.
- However, first person narrators can be **unreliable**, always question whether they are reporting the facts, or their version of the truth.
- Be especially careful if a first person narrator is reporting something that another character has told them, as this becomes a story within a story, and they are likely to apply some **bias** during their version of events.

Third Person Narrators

- A third person narrator is **not directly involved** within the world of the text. As a result, they can report on the thoughts and actions of any number of characters.
- As third person narrators are not directly involved with other characters or within the plot, they have less reason to report in a biased way. Third person narrators are **usually considered to be more reliable**, having said that, be careful, as they usually present certain characters in a more favourable light than others, they're **not necessarily impartial**.

Eye-witnesses and Speakers in Non-fiction

- An eye-witness testimony may be presented in non-fiction, often in order to 'prove' a point. Be wary of eye-witnesses and treat them in the same way as first person narrators. They can be trusted to give their own version of events, based on their emotions and observations, but they are **not reliable in providing definitive facts**.
- Speakers in non-fiction texts may be talking from personal experience, if this is the case, it's likely that they want to promote a particular point of view. If they are using the first person, **be wary** about accepting what they say as the truth, the whole truth and nothing but the truth.
- If a speaker in non-fiction has adopted an **impersonal tone** this is a good indication that they are intending to present a more objective account.

Discourse Markers

Writers use discourse markers to enable them to create a text structure that is accessible, clear and easy to follow.

Compare, Contrast and Qualify

- Discourse markers such as 'similarly', 'likewise', 'in the same way' and 'equally' allow a writer to show that they are drawing a **comparison between two points**.
- Discourse markers such as 'conversely', 'contrary' and 'on the other hand' enable a writer to **highlight contrasting points**.
- Discourse markers such as 'however', 'although' and 'despite' help to show that a comparison or contrast may **need qualification** in order to make a point that will stand up to scrutiny.
- Compare, contrast and qualify discourse markers are often to be found in texts that seek to present an argument or persuade the reader into agreeing to a particular point of view.

Sequencing and Cause & Effect

- Ordinals such as 'firstly' and 'secondly', plus discourse markers such as 'next' and 'after that' allow writers to show that their points should be read in a **specific order**.
- Discourse markers such as 'If... then' and 'consequently' show that there is an element of **cause and effect** in the points that are being made.
- These kinds of discourse markers can be found in fiction texts if a writer wants to show that a character's actions have had consequences.

Illustration and Emphasis

- Discourse markers such as 'for example' or 'illustrated by' allow a writer to tell their reader that they are **about to provide evidence** for the points they are making.
- Discourse markers such as 'most notably', 'of paramount importance' and 'most significantly' enable writers to emphasise a particular point so that it **stands out** above all others.
- These forms of discourse markers are particularly useful to writers who want to present a review.

Sentence Forms and Paragraph Forms

Writers make active decisions when it comes to choosing sentence forms and paragraphs forms in order to convey their ideas in a precise way and create specific effects.

Simple Sentence

- A simple sentence has a verb and a subject, these make up a clause, the clause can stand alone in conveying one complete piece of information.
- Simple sentences increase the pace in a piece of writing, this in turn can help to build tension. They can also be used to add clarity.
  'I collected the tickets.'

Sentence Fragments

- A fragment lacks at least one element that would make it a simple sentence.
- Fragments can be particularly useful if a writer wants to add tension and realism into direct speech.
  'Stop!'

Complex Sentence

- A complex sentence is when a main clause is supported by at least one subordinate clause.
- Complex sentences will allow writers to elaborate upon an idea or argument.
  'Standing in the doorway, I collected the tickets.'

Compound Sentence

- A compound sentence is when two or more clauses are linked by connectives.
- Compound sentences will allow writers to add detail and draw comparisons.
  'I collected the tickets, and I showed people to their seats.'

Paragraphs

- Short paragraphs will make key information stand out.
  'Finally, I'd been given the leading role.'
- Longer paragraphs will allow writers to add detail and develop ideas.
  'That first day at school was overwhelming. Not only did I have to learn every person's name, I also had to try to work out what they were like. Who was vicious, who was vain. Who I could trust and who to avoid.'

Paragraph order

- Controlled paragraph order should complement the overall text structure, for example, if a writer wanted to create a chronological structure, they would ensure that their paragraphs didn't jump forwards and backwards in time.

Developing Answers

- When you answer a reading question, begin by making a **point**. Points are formed of your responses, ideas and opinions about the text. Keep points focused and precise.
- Once you've made your point, you need to prove that what you're saying is valid by using **evidence** from the text, in the form of a quotation. Keep quotations as short as possible.
- Once you've given your evidence, **explain** how this proves your initial point. In your explanation, you should go into detail and develop your answer as much as possible.
- In the higher mark questions, when you progress on to your next point, you should try and **link** it to the previous point, as this will add further development to your response.
- Linking points is especially important when you are completing questions where you have to compare and contrast texts.
- It might help to remember this method as **P.E.E.L.** Point, Evidence, Explain, Link.

Using Quotations

- In your responses to the reading questions, you must use **quotations** to **prove** the validity of the points that you make.
- Each time you make a **new point**, you need **new evidence** from the text.
- Try and keep the quotations you use as **short** as possible, this increases the likelihood of providing focused evidence and cuts down on the time you spend copying out pieces of the text.
- Ideally, you should try to **blend your quotes** into the flow of the point you are making. This is usually achieved by using quotes that are just one or two words long.
- When you do quote from the text, ensure that you copy it **accurately**, pay particular attention to the spelling and punctuation in the quote.
- Always use inverted commas around the text that you are quoting.

Become a clock-watcher! Many students fail to plan their time in an exam. The danger is obvious: unanswered questions = lower grade.

Reading Section - Fiction

Blacknock Sands

     Stiffkey saltmarsh is a shifting landscape, pieced together with drab brown mounds of mud, mellow gold sandbanks and swathes of low growing plants. All of this is shot through with rivulets of seawater. The air smells of seaweed, and is filled with the cries of terns and curlews.

5   Women can be seen toiling on the saltmarsh; one has strayed further out than the others. Bent double, they rake the mud for 'Stookey Blues', the best cockles in the country.

     They're swaddled in sacking to guard against the cold, but their young faces are already leather, tanned by wind and salt.

10   One of the women looks up. She lets out a cry. The rest of the group follow her gaze and realise that a white wall of fog is roiling in off the sea.

     They groan and throw their rakes into half-filled baskets, irritated that they'll only get half-pay.

     'Nancy. Fog's here,' one of them shouts to the lone worker.

15   Nancy points to her half-filled basket then continues with her work.

     'Don't be so soft, leave that and get home to your baby.'

     Nancy deliberately turns her back on the others and digs into the silt with vicious little blows. She's used to half-pay, hunger and cold, but her baby isn't and she wants it to stay that way.

20   In the end, the woman shrugs and follows the other cockle girls back to the village.

     Nancy ranges further and further across the marsh, by the time she's filled her basket she's on Blacknock Sandbank, but in the mist, she can't tell.

     Nancy starts to head home. She thinks she's going in the right direction but the

25 mist shrouds every feature of the landscape in a wrapping of pale grey.

     Soon, Nancy finds that her way is barred by a swollen stream. The current is surging inland. She's left it very late to beat this greedy tide. She looks about but the airy blank of fog hides all.

     Nancy starts to hasten alongside the water, hoping to find a crossing… it

30 wouldn't make any difference though, she's heading in the wrong direction: heading out to sea.

     Now, in the distance can be heard splashing oars and the shouts of men.

     'Where are you love? Nancy?' Nancy's heart clenches with relief.

     'Here, I'm over here.' She calls out then listens for a reply, as she waits she has to

35 edge up the sandbank to stay on dry land. With voices muted by the mist, the men continue to shout, but their calls are not in response to Nancy's cries. Their voices grow fainter again.

     She is now trapped on a mound of sand. The current is hungry and she can feel the sand being sucked out from under her feet, pulling her down. Another minute and

40 the mount is under water. She braces her legs and calls out again.

     Holding her basket of cockles makes her unbalanced; reluctantly she sacrifices it to the water. The driving current devours it without hesitation.

     Her skirts balloon around her waist, held aloft on the surface of the biting cold water. She knows she should save her breath and try to swim but she wastes it calling

45 out again and again.

     Momentarily, one of the men in the rescue boat thinks he catches a keening voice on the air but then he can't be sure, and afterwards all he hears is the cry of a curlew.

Reading Section - Fiction

Life of a Seafood Salesman

Frankie Goes to Hollywood was telling people to 'Relax' and Jason Jones had taken this advice to heart. It was week five of his summer job, and so far, nobody had discovered that he spent much of his working day hiding out on the flat roof of the amusements arcade. Instead of selling seafood from a little cart, he would sunbathe,
5 read and eavesdrop on holiday-makers.

Jason was supposed to circulate round Butlin's, selling cockles and mussels, but he'd quickly worked out that regardless of how much he sold, he still got paid.

Never before had Jason Jones had so much money. He felt he'd invested it sensibly by buying himself a Swatch Watch and some stone washed jeans, as well as
10 having his hair permed in order to look like superstar footballer, Kevin Keegan. Jason's older brother declared that the perm was 'bogus' but Jason's friends wisely confirmed that it was extremely cool.

From his vantage point on top of the arcade, Jason could see the entrance to *The Pig and Whistle*, one of Butlin's many bars. If he saw a big group of punters going
15 in, he'd give them about an hour, then head on over with his seafood.

The interior of *The Pig and Whistle* was garish, like a working man's club in fancy dress, decorated with an eclectic mixture of junk shop tat.

Today, there was a big group of people sitting round the table closest to the stage. Even though it was only midday, their table was already cluttered with empties.
20 Jason wheeled over to them, picking up their London accents.

''ere mate, wotcha selling?' asked a sunburnt bloke the size of Big Daddy.

'Mussels, cockles, whelks…'

'Eww, whelks,' said the woman sitting closest to Mr Sunburn.

'Whelks! Lovely, watch this love!' He grabbed one of the little polystyrene pots of
25 whelks. A chorus of 'Down it! down it!' started up from the other guys round the table. The women squealed in disgust as Mr Sunburn tilted his head back and tipped all of the whelks down his gaping gullet in one go.

After that, sales came thick and fast, as every bloke wanted to outdo the others, until every jellied eel and crab stick had been consumed.
30 Jason started to push his trolley back to the kitchens to get a refill.

'Hi Jason.' Jason looked over to see his friend Darren.

'Hey Darren, want to race? I'll race you to the kitchens.' Jason shot off, laughing. The trolley's little wheels clattered over the concrete and the lid bounced about, enjoying the ride.
35 Jason sneaked a peak over his shoulder to see that Darren was close on his heels. He swerved in close to a flowerbed to force Darren to pull up sharp. Darren put on a spurt of speed in order to make it through the gap.

Daring though it was, Darren's move did not work out. His trolley skidded on a stone then swerved uncontrollably into the flowers. Upended, it spewed out the
40 remnants of a prawn cocktail that had been hiding at the bottom. Pink sauce and prawns now spattered the regimented white bedding flowers.

Jason stopped and turned to survey the disaster he'd left in his wake, then looked up at Darren. Both boys burst out laughing. Between guffaws, Jason managed to get enough breathe to do an impression of Sean Connery, shouting out 'Prawn cocktails,
45 shaken not stirred,' to the crowd of holiday-makers that had gathered. Needless to say, the boys were marched off the premises that afternoon and told not to bother turning up for work the next day, and with one week of the summer holidays left… it really was time to relax.

Reading Section - Non - Fiction

The Tears of Ra

Ancient Egyptian mythology tells us that when the sun god Ra wept, and his tears fell upon the desert, they did not soak into the burning sand, instead, they transformed into bees.

Our ancient ancestors can be forgiven for worshiping bees and for using honey, but
5   3000 years on, it's time to re-examine our beliefs. Honey is not a magical elixir gifted to humans, it's made by bees, for bees.

What does it take to make honey?

Worker bees collect flower nectar, process it in their bodies then transport it back to the hive where they regurgitate it. This liquid is then processed again as bees chew the
10 nectar in order to add enzymes, before fanning it with their wings to reduce the water content, thus forming it into the substance we know as honey.

Why do bees need honey?

Honey is the food that bees depend upon; it is especially vital to them during the barren winter months when they are unable to forage for nectar.

15 When honey is harvested, the bee farmer will replace it with sugar syrup and although this provides the bees with energy, it cannot compete with the nutritional benefits of honey. Honey has a particular chemical profile that enables bees to maintain a healthy immune system, helping them to deal with pests, pathogens and poisons.

Commercial honey

20 Commercial honey is produced using methods seen elsewhere in the factory farming world. For example, selective breeding is used to produce bees that are more docile than their wild counterparts, rendering them easier to farm. Selective breeding is a death sentence for the drones as they are killed during the procedure, while the queen bees are artificially inseminated, thus violating them in the process.

25 Many bee farmers choose to exterminate their colonies at the end of the summer season as this can be more cost effective than tending them over the winter. Preferred methods for destroying bees include incinerating the hives with the bees trapped inside, or pumping cyanide gas into the colony.

The honey industry treats living creatures as mere commodities and exploits them in
30 order to make money.

Bad for bees, bad for you

In recent times, there has been a big drive to reduce the amount of sugar in our diets and considering honey is essentially sugar, it makes sense to cut it out.

Scientists have also found that a lot of honey is now contaminated with
35 neonicotinoids, which are chemical pesticides used in the agricultural industry. Do you really want to be consuming these?

Not your hive, not your honey

Ultimately, every individual has to make their own ethical choices, but giving up honey isn't a difficult one. There are so many plant based alternatives: molasses, golden
40 syrup and agave nectar to name a few.

Bees aren't the Tears of Ra, they're living creatures, social creatures, creatures that have been observed as exhibiting feelings of sadness and pessimism. Do you really want to strip them of their essential food source, one they've laboured all their short lives to produce, just so you can have a sweet treat?

Plan Bee

Be beautiful

Plan Bee is *the* new haircare range that will leave you buzzing. It harnesses the properties of honey in order to give you beautiful, healthy hair. Honey's antibacterial
5 qualities deliver superior cleansing for hair and scalp. Naturally occurring emollients lock in moisture, leaving hair shiny. Bioactive features strengthen follicles and replenish keratin fibres, especially good for those with thinning hair. The unique ingredients in honey will enhance gold tones, leaving blondes blonder, brunettes burnished and red-heads radiant.
10

Plan Bee products are hand crafted. Honey is combined with other natural ingredients, such as oat milk, to deliver a range that retains the authentic, sweet aroma of its key ingredient.

15 ### Be ethical

For thousands of years, humans have prized honey for its taste and for its therapeutic qualities. In modern times, commercial honey farming has led to unethical bee-keeping practices and low quality products. Plan Bee seeks to redress this situation by
20 returning to ancient methods, which take a bee-centred approach, and as a result, bring the consumer a range of genuinely beneficial, ethical, honey based haircare products.

Plan Bee curates an apiary of 35 hives, which are situated in an organically managed
25 landscape. Our bees are free to forage on a diverse range of nectar rich plants, including clover, honeysuckle and lavender.

It is our philosophy to facilitate natural bee behaviour. We do not, for instance, clip the wings of our queen bees, this leaves them free to swarm away if they choose. Nor do
30 we pump our hives full of antibiotics regardless of whether the bees need medical attention or not.

When Plan Bee does harvest honey, it is all done with the utmost respect for the bees and we only take honey when there is a plentiful supply.
35

Plan Bee can guarantee that its haircare range is cruelty free as none of the products have ever been tested on animals.

Plan Bee is serious about protecting the welfare of bees and actively lobbies the British
40 parliament in order to bring about a total ban on the use of all insecticides suspected of contributing to Colony Collapse Disorder. In addition, we contribute 20% of all profits to environmental charities that focus on developing our understand of apian culture.

We believe that our ethos enables the consumer to buy with confidence. Confidence
45 in the efficacy of our range and confidence in the fact that it has come from a cruelty free background. There's certainly no sting at the end of this tale.

Reading Skills: Assessment Objective 1

Assessment Objective 1

This objective tests your ability to:
- **Identify** explicit information/ideas, **interpret** implicit information/ideas.
- **Select** evidence from different texts and **synthesise** this evidence.

Exam tips for AO1

- If your exam question directs you to focus on a **specific section** of the text, you MUST take your answers from this section in order to gain the marks on offer.
- Use a highlighter to mark the boundaries of the specific section to help you stay focused.

Sample Questions

The following questions are in reference to the text 'Blacknock Sands'.

1. **Look again at lines 1 to 4.**
   List four features of the saltmarsh environment. [4]
2. **Look at lines 5 to 9.**
   How do the women stand when they are harvesting the shellfish? [1]
   How do you know that the women always work out in the open? [1]
   What does this tell you about the kind of lives the women lead? [1]
3. **Look from the beginning of the text to line 14.**
   Out of the following statements, which four are TRUE: [4]
   a) The air smells of seaweed.
   b) There are a few trees growing on the saltmarshes.
   c) You can hear the sound of seabirds.
   d) The women are digging for cockles called 'Stookey Blues'.
   e) The women are old.
   f) The women are pleased when they see the fog approaching.
   g) The women are working in one big group.
   h) The women are wrapped in sacks.
4. **Focus on lines 5 to 17.** Identify two ways in which the writer shows that Nancy is a loner. [2]
5. **Reread lines 24 to 28.**
   Select two quotations that describe the sea fog. [2]

The following questions are in reference to 'Blacknock Sands' and 'Life of a Salesman'.

6. Identify key similarities shared by Nancy and Jason. [2]
7. Summarise the differences between Nancy and Jason. [8]

Assessment Objective 1 - Responses

1. **Look again at lines 1 to 4. List four features of the saltmarsh environment. [4]**
   You could choose up to four of the following: i) shifting landscape, ii) has mounds of mud, iii) has sandbanks, iv) has rivulets of seawater, v) air smells of seaweed, vi) is home to seabirds like terns and curlews.

2. **Look at lines 5 to 9. How do the women stand when they are harvesting the shellfish? [1]**
   They stand 'bent double' when they harvest cockles.
   How do you know that the women always work out in the open? [1]
   Their skin has been weather beaten 'tanned by wind and salt'.
   What does this tell you about the kind of lives the women lead? [1]
   The women lead hard lives because they have to do backbreaking work from a young age.

3. **Look from the beginning of the text to line 14. Out of the following statements, which four are TRUE: [4]**
   a) The air smells of seaweed.
   c) You can hear the sound of seabirds.
   d) The women are digging for cockles called 'Stookey Blues'.
   h) The women are wrapped in sacks.

4. **Focus on lines 5 to 17. Identify two ways in which the writer shows that Nancy is a loner. [2]**
   Nancy has chosen to work apart from the main group 'one has strayed further out than the others'.
   Nancy refuses to return to the village with the other cockle pickers 'Nancy deliberately turns her back on the others'.

5. **Reread lines 24 to 28. Select 2 quotations that describe the sea fog. [2]**
   The fog is described as a 'shroud', a 'wrapping of pale grey' and as an 'airy blank'.

6. **Identify key similarities shared by Nancy and Jason. [2]**
   Nancy and Jason are both young and Nancy and Jason both have a job.

7. **Summarise the differences between the working life of Nancy and Jason. [8]**
   Nancy has to work in order to earn money to keep herself and her baby alive, she is determined never to let her child go hungry, whereas Jason is only working in order to earn some pocket money. Jason has been able to fritter away his money on non-essential consumer items such as his 'Swatch Watch' as well as other unnecessary expenditure such as his 'perm'.

   Nancy's working conditions are cold and harsh, even though all the cockle pickers are young, their faces 'are already leather, tanned by wind and salt', whereas Jason's working conditions are extremely easy. He's worked out that he can get away with spending most of his day 'hiding out', and not doing anything.

   Nancy seems to have excluded herself from the company of the other cockle pickers 'one has strayed further out than the others', suggesting she is determined to put all her efforts into work and is not prepared to waste even the smallest amount of effort on being sociable. On the other hand, Jason actively enjoys mucking around with other Butlin's employees, for instance, he is the one who instigates the seafood cart dash that ends in disaster.

   At the end of 'Life of a Seafood Salesman' Jason loses his job and although this might seem like negative result, Jason doesn't seem to mind and embraces the chance to spend the last week of his summer holiday just relaxing. In contrast, at the end of 'Blacknock Sands' the text implies that Nancy loses her life as a result of her employment.

Reading Skills: Assessment Objective 2

Assessment Objective 2

This objective tests your ability to:

- **Analyse** how writers use language and structure to create effects and influence readers.
- Use **technical terminology** to clarify your analysis.

Exam tips for AO2

- AO2 question may direct you to focus on a specific section of the text, if so, you MUST take your answers from this section in order to gain the marks on offer.
- If directed to use a specific section, use a highlighter to mark its boundaries to help you stay focused.
- Alternatively, AO2 questions may direct you to use the whole text, so read your question carefully.
- AO2 questions may direct you to focus on just the language, just the structure, or tell you to analyse both, ensure you respond to what the question is asking.
- You must use evidence to support your analysis of the text.
- Blending short, carefully chosen quotations into your writing is an effective way to do this.
- Do not copy out long sections of the text in order to quote, this wastes time and can lead to answers that are imprecise.
- When asked to analyse language, the following are key areas to consider: vocabulary choices, word class, phrases, sentence forms, figurative language, rhetoric, idioms, direct speech.
- When asked to analyse structure, the following are key areas to consider: beginnings, endings, turning points, changes in viewpoint/narrator, repetition of ideas, order of events, paragraphing.
- Using technical terminology is a must and will help you to deliver perceptive answers.

Sample Questions

These questions are in reference to the text 'Blacknock Sands'.

1. **Look at lines 10 to 14.** How does the writer use language to show that the fog is dangerous? [2]
2. Look at the whole text, how is language used to show that cockle picking is hard work? [6]
3. Look at the whole text, analyse how the writer uses language and structure to create tension. [12]

These questions are in reference to the text 'Life of a Seafood Salesman'.

4. How does the writer use structure to highlight Jason's attitude to work? [4]
5. How does the writer use language to create a light-hearted, entertaining tone in the text? [8]

Assessment Objective 2 - Responses

1. **Look at lines 10 to 14. How does the writer use language to show that the fog is dangerous? [2]**

   The first woman to see the fog lets of a 'cry' suggesting she is alarmed by the sight of it. She alerts the others to the fog suggesting it is something to be feared.
   The fog is described as a 'wall', which emphasises that it is so thick, you can't see through it. It is also described as 'roiling' suggesting that it is highly agitated, giving the impression that it is fast moving, this also personifies it as angry.

2. **How is language used to show that cockle picking is hard work? [6]**

   Initially, the women are described as 'toiling' this immediately tells the reader that the work is hard.
   The women have to be 'bent double' in order to rake up the cockles, this shows their work is physically hard.
   The women are 'swaddled in sacking', this shows that they do not really have adequate clothing to be working in a cold environment, therefore, they have to work in uncomfortable conditions.
   Even though they are young, their faces have been 'tanned by salt and wind' suggesting that they have been expected to undertake this hard work from a young age.
   The women only have hand 'rakes' as implements, they do not have any machinery to make their job easier.
   The women walk back to the village, this implies that they do not have any kind of animals or transportation to help them get out to the cockle beds or back from them when they are laden with full, heavy baskets.

Don't be shy about your work. Get your friends/family/teacher to read over your practise answers. Ask them what you need to do to improve.

Assessment Objective 2 - Responses

3. Analyse how the writer uses language and structure to create tension. [12]

Throughout the text, the forces of nature are described as posing a threat in order to create tension.

Right from the start, the reader is taught that the fog is something to be feared as when the woman sees it, she 'lets out a cry' of alarm.

The weather is described as a 'wall of fog', this imagery suggests that it's so dense, air and water have become solid, giving the impression that it's impossibly thick and therefore something you need to get away from.

Later, the reader is told that the mist 'shrouds' every feature and this alludes to a theme of death, thus increasing the tension.

As the action progresses, the fog is joined by another natural threat, that of the rising tide. The tide is personified with words such as 'greedy', 'hungry', 'devours' and 'biting'. This lexical field makes it seem like the tide is a hunter with Nancy being its prey.

Throughout the text, the language and structure is used to show that Nancy is isolated from everyone else. Right at the beginning, the reader is told that 'one has strayed further out than the others'. This foreshadows the situation later, where Nancy is lost and alone on Blacknock Sandbank.

Unlike all the other cockle pickers, Nancy makes the decision to stay out on the marsh. As she carries on digging, she does so with 'vicious little blows' to show that she is distraught about having to make the difficult choice between getting home safely or continuing with her risky work in order to earn enough money to feed her baby.

Lines 29 to 31 bring dramatic irony as they confirm that Nancy is heading in the wrong direction but that she is unaware of this.

Just when the reader fears that Nancy is going to be trapped out on the marsh, the sound of the men in the rescue boat is introduced into the structure of the narrative, giving hope that Nancy will be saved. However, this hope is short-lived as the men can't find her in the mist and row away without her.

It is poignant that Nancy 'sacrifices' her full basket of cockles to the rising waters, as if she does somehow survive, all her struggles will have been in vain and this enhances the pathos of the story.

In the final paragraph, one of the rescuers 'thinks he catches a keening voice on the air', making it seem like Nancy will be found after all, but this is undermined by the fact that in the end, all he can hear is the 'cry of a curlew'.

This reference to the seabird refers the reader back to the opening paragraph where they are told that the air is filled with 'the cries of terns and curlews'. This suggests that nature carries on with its own affairs, unaware and uncaring of any human tragedy.

At the end, it's never confirmed whether Nancy does indeed perish, or is rescued somehow. This ending leaves the reader wondering about her fate, so the story will continue to play on their mind.

Assessment Objective 2 - Responses

4. How does the writer use structure to highlight Jason's attitude to work? [4]

'Life of a Seafood Salesman' begins by explaining that Jason spends much of his working day relaxing on the 'flat roof of the amusements arcade'; by presenting this information at the start of the text, the writer is communicating that it has the most significance and that Jason's attitude to work revolves around doing as little as possible.

As the text progresses, it reveals how Jason manages to get away with doing very little. The scene in The Pig and Whistle shows that Jason understands how to get a lot of sales made in a short space of time, leaving him free to return to his sunbathing, reading and eavesdropping. This shows that Jason's attitude to work is to be smart, not dogged.

After Jason has made his sales in the pub, he is shown instigating the trolley race with his friend, suggesting that he is in no rush to make any more sales in the immediate future, which is very much in keeping with the relaxed attitude that was introduced right at the beginning of the text.

In the final paragraph, Jason sees being sacked as a good thing because it will give him more time to 'relax', emphasising once again that his attitude to work is consistently laid back.

5. How does the writer use language and structure to make the text light-hearted and entertaining? [8]

The text begins with a reference to a classic 80's pop song that immediately establishes a fun, informal tone.

The text gently mocks Jason with a touch of sarcasm, he feels that buying clothes and getting a perm is investing his wages 'sensibly' and has no concept of what it really means to invest in a serious, adult way.

Jason's friends 'wisely' confirm that his hair looks 'extremely cool', this is juxtaposed with the reality that a schoolboy with a perm is likely to look anything but 'cool'. The dramatic irony here is that the modern reader knows his 80's hair looks funny, whereas, Jason sports his look without any sense of irony.

The Mr Sunburn character adds a light-hearted element to the text as despite his self-inflicted injuries, he's determined to have fun by going to the pub and showing off when he eats the whelks.

When Mr Sunburn's friends start chanting 'Down it! down it!' this adds to the sense of entertainment as they are not simply eating seafood, they've made it into a game of daring.

When Jason and Darren have the race, their trolleys are personified. The fact that Jason's trolley is 'enjoying' the race enhances the joyous tone because it's as if it's been animated by Jason's sense of fun. At the culmination of the race, Darren's trolley 'spewed' out the prawn cocktail, making it seem like a little child who has got so excited they've been sick.

Jason's allusion to the James Bond catchphrase 'shaken not stirred' creates comedy as the image of prawn cocktail spattered all over Butlin's is in complete opposition to the suave, sophisticated image of the super spy.

The text concludes with Jason being sacked, however, he is happy about this as he sees it as yet another opportunity to 'relax'. This leaves the reader feeling confident that they do not have to worry about Jason, whatever happens to him, he will deal with it in a light-hearted way.

Reading Skills: Assessment Objective 3

Assessment Objective 3

This objective tests your ability to:
- **Compare** ideas and perspectives.
- **Compare** how writers present their ideas and perspectives.

Exam tips for AO3

- AO3 questions require you to compare texts, so ensure this is the focus of your answer.
- You MUST respond to both texts in order to access the full range of marks.
- You might like to draw up a table of similarities/differences in order to help you approach this kind of question.
- Try to alternate between the texts, in order to give a balanced answer. If you find yourself starting to focus too much on one text, you've probably lost sight of that core comparison element.
- When the question asks you to compare the 'methods', here are some key areas to look at:

i)   The form, purpose and audience. For example, are the texts intended for a public or private audience? Do they aim to inform/entertain/review?
ii) What is their tone? Is one more serious/light-hearted than the other?
iii) Compare their use of language by looking at: vocabulary choices, word class, phrases, sentence forms, figurative language, rhetoric, idioms, and direct speech.
iv) Compare their use of structure by looking at: beginnings, endings, turning points, changes in viewpoint/narrator, repetition of ideas, order of events, and paragraphing.

- You must use evidence to support your comparisons.
- Ensure your use of evidence is balanced across both texts and that it clarifies the points for comparison that you are making.

Sample Questions

1. Look at 'The Tears of Ra' and 'Plan Bee' then compare how the writers view using honey. [6]

2. Look at the texts 'Blacknock Sands' and 'Life of a Seafood Salesman' then compare the presentation of Nancy and Jason in the two fiction texts. [6]

3. Using 'The Tears of Ra' and 'Plan Bee', compare how the writers present their ideas about bees and honey. [14]

Assessment Objective 3 - Responses

1. Compare how the writers view using honey. [6]

Both the writers have very passionate ideas about keeping bees and using honey, however, they differ in their perspectives.

The writer of 'The Tears of Ra' is adamant that honey is 'made by bees, for bees' and that any human interference in this process is cruel, exploitative and unacceptable.

On the other hand, the writer of 'Plan Bee' promotes the idea that as long as a bee-keeper facilitates 'natural bee behaviour' it is acceptable to keep them and use honey, as long as it's done in a humane, responsible way.

The writer of 'The Tears of Ra' sees no reason to use honey as there are 'so many plant based alternatives', and presents giving up honey as an easy ethical choice.

In contrast, the writer of 'Plan Bee' perceives honey to be a particularly potent product, with its 'Bioactive features', they see it as something for which there is no substitute. Therefore, they are prepared to go to a lot of trouble, curating the hives in the 'organically managed landscape' in order to produce a supply of honey.

2. Compare the presentation of Nancy and Jason in the two fiction texts. [6]

Both characters seem to exhibit traits that could be considered characteristic of young people.

Nancy's youth and lack of experience may be one of the reasons why she makes the fateful decision to carry on working, even after she has been informed that the 'Fog's here'.

Jason sometimes seems to behave in a carefree, even irresponsible way. Not only does he spend 'much of his working day hiding out on the flat roof of the amusements arcade', he also ends up causing havoc in the workplace when he instigates the trolley race. It could be argued that his daring attitude is in keeping with his youthfulness.

So, although both characters exhibit signs of being young, these affect their behaviour in very different ways.

Both characters also have traits that make them seem older and wiser than their years.

Although Nancy is young, she has to behave in an extremely mature, adult way, as she already has the huge responsibility of supporting her 'baby'. She takes motherhood very seriously and this drives her to work hard for a living.

Jason shows that despite his youth, he has a canny and perceptive understand of human behaviour, he knows that by giving the holiday makers 'about an hour' in the pub, they will work up an appetite for snacks, meaning that he can make a lot of sales in an efficient way, in a short amount of time.

Both characters are presented as sympathetic. Although Nancy seems taciturn, her sense of responsibility makes the reader warm to her, while Jason is clearly a very likeable character with his clever personality and good humour.

Assessment Objective 3 - Responses

3. Compare how the writers present their ideas about bees and honey. [14]

Both writers have a serious message at the heart of their writing, however, they convey this in different ways.

The writer of 'The Tears of Ra' never deviates from using a serious tone, information such as 'bee farmers choose to exterminate their colonies' creates a grim mood and this is done to impress upon the reader their view, which is that keeping bees is cruel.

On the other hand, although 'Plan Bee' is serious in its own way, it has light-hearted elements. For example the use of the pun 'leave you buzzing', (referencing both the noise of bees and a sense of joy in the consumer) communicates the fact that the writer is being playful as well serious.

Both writers have distilled their key messages into slogans, which they use as headings. In 'The Tears of Ra' maxims such as 'Not your hive, not your honey' succinctly conveys the idea that honey is not for human consumption, while in 'Plan Bee', the two headings 'Be beautiful' and 'Be ethical' also act as a slogan, and inform the reader about the two key aspects of the haircare range.

Both writers pick up on the theme that the relationship between humans and bees ranges far back into history. 'The Tears of Ra' uses this to advocate that 'it's time to re-examine' our use of honey and in doing so, realise that it is outdated, before turning to 'plant based alternatives'. In contrast, 'Plan Bee' suggests that it is only in modern times that bee keeping has become unethical, but that a return to 'ancient methods' will facilitate ethical honey farming.

Both writers use highly emotive language in order to shock readers into accepting their ideas and perspectives. 'The Tears of Ra' tells the reader that 'Selective breeding is a death sentence for the drones' and 'Plan Bee' reveals that they do not 'clip the wings' of their queen bees. Such language is intended to make the reader connect with the issue at an emotional level, and the ensuing feelings should motivate them to reassess their own attitudes.

'The Tears of Ra' uses a vocabulary designed to make honey seem repellent. The idea that bees 'regurgitate' nectar characterises it essentially as vomit, in an attempt to put people off wanting to eat it. Later, the article informs readers that honey is 'contaminated with... chemical pesticides' in order to undermine honey's image as a natural, wholesome product and therefore not at all pleasant to eat.

In contrast, 'Plan Bee' uses a vocabulary that is used to make honey seem attractive. The idea that the bees take nectar from flowers such as 'clover, honeysuckle and lavender' elevates the idea that this is a sweet, fragrant product and therefore desirable.

Both texts use a lexis of scientific language in order to promote their point of view. 'The Tears of Ra' tells the reader that 'Honey has a particular chemical profile that enables bees to maintain a healthy immune system', in order to suggest that they could provide scientific proof as to why bees should be left alone with their honey.

On the other hand, 'Plan Bee' uses a lexis of scientific language in order to make their honey based products attractive to customers. They use jargon such as 'antibacterial', 'emollients', and 'Bioactive features' in order to suggest that they could provide scientific evidence as to why honey is an effective ingredient and should be enjoyed by the consumer.

Both texts use repetition in their final paragraph in order to finish with a lasting message. 'The Tears of Ra' repeats the idea that bees are 'creatures' in order to emphasise the fact that they are not inanimate playthings, while 'Plan Bee' repeats the idea that consumers can have 'confidence' in their haircare products as they are both effective and ethical.

'The Tears of Ra' ends with a final, biting rhetorical question in order to leave the reader thinking about whether they really do need to use honey products. 'Plan Bee' ends with the light hearted comment that there is 'no sting' in their products and this makes the consumer feel comfortable about using honey products.

Reading Skills: Assessment Objective 4

Assessment Objective 4

This objective tests your ability to:
- **Critically evaluate** texts.
- Use **textual evidence** to support your evaluation.

Exam tips for AO4

- Depending upon which exam board you are using, AO4 questions may direct you to use a section of a text, a whole text or even two texts. Ensure that you read your question carefully and focus on what is specified.
- If you are directed to focus on just a section, you may wish to highlight this.
- AO4 questions will either offer an opinion, or make a statement and then ask how far you agree with the point of view.
- In AO4 questions you need to give your opinion about the text.
- Ensure you support your opinions with evidence in order to prove that what you're proposing is credible.
- As always, it is better to use short focused quotes, blended into your own writing, rather than copying out large passages from the text, in order to achieve the best marks possible.
- AO4 questions carry a lot of marks so ensure you have paced yourself so that you have ample time to complete these longer answers.

Sample Questions

1. In 'Blacknock Sands' there is an overwhelming sense of isolation - how far do you agree with this statement?
   * Write about your own impressions of the text.
   * Evaluate how the writer has created the sense of isolation.
   * Use evidence to support your work. [12]

2. In 'Life of a Seafood Salesman' the character of Jason Jones is lively and engaging.
   * Give you opinion about the character of Jason Jones.
   * Evaluate how successfully Jason's character is portrayed.
   * Support your work with evidence from the text. [12]

3. The writer in 'The Tears of Ra' attempts to persuade the reader that humans should not use honey.
   * Evaluate how effective they are in their arguments.
   * Use references to the text in order to support your opinion. [15]

4. Plan Bee sets out to convince consumers that their haircare products are both ethical and effective.
   * Evaluate whether they have been successful in their aims.
   * Use textual references to support your work. [20]

Assessment Objective 4 - Responses

1. **In 'Blacknock Sands' there is an overwhelming sense of isolation - how far do you agree with this statement?**
   * Write about your own impressions of the text.
   * Evaluate how the writer has created the sense of isolation.
   * Use evidence to support your work. [12]

A sense of isolation does dominate 'Blacknock Sands' and is used to engage the reader's emotions.

Initially, the writer establishes that the main character, Nancy, is a solitary person. In the second paragraph the reader is told that Nancy has 'strayed farther out than the others'. This makes her seem both wilful and vulnerable. This characterisation engages the reader making them feel both irritated by and protective over Nancy.

When the other cockle pickers warn Nancy that the 'Fog's here', Nancy chooses not to give a verbal reply, instead she silently 'continues with her work'. This adds to the growing sense that she is isolated from the others, as she will not even speak to them.

This self-exclusion is emphasised even further when Nancy 'deliberately turns her back on the others'. This body language suggests that she has to put a physical barrier between her and the others, as in her heart of hearts she knows it would be sensible to go home with them, however, she is resolved to keep working alone.

The fact that the other woman just 'shrugs' in response to Nancy's silence suggests that she is familiar with such behaviour and has learnt not to waste any effort on persuading Nancy to do anything. This tells the reader that Nancy is a difficult and solitary person by nature, and this proves to be her fatal flaw.

Not only does the sense of isolation come from the characterisation of Nancy, it also comes from the writer's use of setting. The fact that the mist 'shrouds every feature' of the saltmarsh gives the impression of emptiness and of nothingness and evokes a feeling of dread in the mind of the reader.

In the beginning, it had been Nancy's choice to be alone, however, this control is taken from her by the dreadful environment; suddenly, she in no longer solitary by choice, she is lost and trapped, 'she can't tell' where she is.

Through the use of dramatic irony, the reader is told that even though Nancy thinks she's making for home, she's actually 'heading out to sea'. This turn of events creates tension as the reader fears for Nancy, lost and alone in the void of the 'airy blank'.

At this point of crisis, the writer structures the narrative so that it seems like tragedy will be averted, suddenly 'in the distance can be heard splashing oars and the shouts of men'. Nancy is no longer out in the wilderness on her own. Just like Nancy, the reader feels 'relief' that she is no longer isolated.

The fact that a rescue party is looking for her tells the reader that the other cockle pickers, who left early, were worried about Nancy and sent the men out to look for her. The tragedy is that Nancy's self-imposed position of isolation is unnecessary; as far as her community is concerned, they'd like to include her and help her.

The narrative is then structured so that just when it seems hopeful that Nancy will be rescued, this possibility is lost. Despite their best efforts, the rescue party cannot locate Nancy and she is left alone on the sandbank, a solitary prisoner of the tide.

Within the landscape of isolation, another presence begins to make itself known with an increasing sense of identity. The tide is personified with language such as 'greedy', 'hungry' and 'biting'. Nancy is not truly alone on the marsh, however, her company, in the form of the incoming tide, is hostile and paradoxically adds to the growing feeling of isolation.

At the end of the narrative, the reader is left feeling that Nancy's self-imposed isolation was a kind of hubris and that if she had been less proud and asked for help with supporting herself and her baby, she would have received it from the other villagers.

Assessment Objective 4 - Responses

2.   In 'Life of a Seafood Salesman' the character of Jason Jones is lively and engaging.
   * Give your opinion about the character of Jason Jones.
   * Evaluate how successfully Jason's character is portrayed.
   * Support your work with evidence from the text. [12]

The reader is initially engaged by the fact that Jason seems like a laid-back person, he's taken 'to heart' the advice to 'relax'. The fact that he got this advice from a pop song enhances his youthfulness, as well as making him sound like he would be fun and easy to get along with. Having said that, some readers may be irritated by Jason's apparent lack of responsibility.

Over the course of the story, it becomes clear that Jason's ability to stay calm is his defining characteristic, this is emphasised by the final sentence, which tells the reader that on being sacked, Jason sees it as further opportunity to 'relax', leaving the reader with a lasting impression of his composed approach to life. All of this makes him an engaging character, as he seems to be unaffected by the stresses of everyday life and this is something to aspire to.

The reader is told that instead of working, Jason would 'eavesdrop on holiday-makers', this piques their interest because it's fun to see a character engaging in mischievous behaviour. It also adds a more dynamic dimension to his character that balances out his generally laid-back attitude.

It appears that Jason has learnt by watching and listening to the holiday-makers. As a result, he is savvy enough to give people 'an hour' in the pub, in order to work up an appetite, before going in and plying his trade, this way, his sales come 'thick and fast'.

This explains why he is able to spend much of his working day 'hiding out on the flat roof of the amusements' as he has worked out how to make a decent amount of money in a short space of time with minimum effort, all because he's using an understanding of human psychology to his advantage. In this respect, he is somewhat of a role model as he is working 'smarter' not 'harder', something that many people strive for in order to have a more productive yet enjoyable lifestyle.

The fact that Jason has spent his wages on a 'Swatch Watch and some stone washed jeans' suggests he is confident, outgoing and likes to be in touch with the world around him, all of which adds to the idea that he is likeable.

Furthermore, he's also taken the daring step of having a 'perm' in order to look like his idol 'Kevin Keegan'. This shows, not only an interest in football, something that many people can relate to, but also that he is a passionate person who admires others.

It is significant that Jason's friends deem his daring hairdo as 'extremely cool', as this intimates that they look up to him, adding to his air of charisma.

When Jason challenges Darren to the trolley race, he is showing his lively side and when he 'swerved in close to a flowerbed' in order to prevent Darren from overtaking him, he also reveals that he does have quite a competitive streak.

After the trolley crash, instead of trying to cover up the incident, or run away, Jason reveals yet another side to his personality, his witty impression shows that he is an entertainer, which again adds to his lively persona.

In a short space of time, the reader gets a clear impression of a character who has many facets, all of which make him seem lively and engaging.

Before you start a revision session, think back over what you covered previously. Can you remember the key points you looked at? If not, spend some time going back over the material before starting a new topic.

Assessment Objective 4 - Responses

3. **The writer in 'The Tears of Ra' attempts to persuade the reader that humans should not use honey.**
   * Evaluate how effective they are in their arguments.
   * Use references to the text in order to support your opinion. [15]

This article goes a long way to persuading people that they should stop eating honey, however, there are problems with the argument that may aggravate some readers rather than persuading them.

The writer opens the article with the ancient Egyptian myth about how bees were created, this is a compelling tale and it's likely to make the audience want to read on. This is closely followed with the point that 'it's time to re-examine our beliefs' about using honey, implying that it's an outdated practice that should be confined to history, and that it has no place in a modern society. This seems like a reasonable statement, and introduces the idea that the writer is presenting a reasonable argument.

This opening argument finishes with the slogan 'it's made by bees, for bees', the pithiness of this statement makes it seem a bit more assertive than the opening paragraphs, and although it is a catchy slogan, it may be off-putting to some readers if they sense they are letting themselves in for a sermon by reading any further.

Having said that, the writer does not pursue a preaching tone at this point, instead, they use the intriguing heading 'What does it take to make honey?' this is effective as a reader's curiosity will encourage them to read on.

This section is effective because although the honey making process is presented factually, it actually has an emotive effect upon the reader. Once they realise that bees 'regurgitate' nectar and 'chew' it over, it suddenly seems less appealing. Therefore, the writer has used facts to support their goal in persuading people to stop eating honey.

In the following section, 'Why do bees need honey?', the writer presents statements such as sugar syrup 'cannot compete with the nutritional benefits of honey' and although this sounds convincing, the writer fails to back this up with any scientific evidence. If only they had cited some research, it would have strengthened such a claim.

In this section the writer starts to introduce emotive language such as 'depend upon' and 'vital', all of which is designed to make the reader feel guilty about taking such a precious resource from the bees; because the emotive language in this section is controlled, it appears subtle and therefore effective.

The next section, 'Commercial honey', increases the emotive content of the writing by telling the reader that selective breeding is a 'death sentence' for the drones and that it is 'violating' to the queen bees. Although some readers may be moved by this information, others may perceive the suggestion that a bee can be violated as far-fetched, in which case, they may feel less inclined to take the article seriously.

The writer persists with the highly emotive content, going on to explain how bee farmers often 'choose to exterminate their colonies', before highlighting two ways in which this is done, both of which are horrifying. To some readers, this may be the final piece of evidence than convinces them to stop eating honey, however, others many find the idea so upsetting that they have to stop reading the article and force the issue out of their mind although because it is too painful to think about.

Assessment Objective 4 - Responses

Answer to question 3 continued...

Despite the upsetting emotional content of the 'Commercial honey' section, it does enlighten the general consumer, and by educating them, the writer is likely to put some of them off buying honey again.

After this highly emotional section, the writer changes tack in order to focus on how honey is not only 'Bad for bees,' but also 'bad for you' too. This is effective because even if the reader is unmoved by the welfare of bees, they are likely to be a lot more interested in their own health.

In this section, the writer uses the logical argument that 'considering honey is essentially sugar' it's in keeping with health conscious trends to omit it from a modern diet.

The writer goes on to make the alarming statement that honey is 'contaminated with neonicotinoids' in order to undermine the 'natural', 'healthy' image that honey trades upon Such statements are likely to put many readers off eating honey, so it is effective. However, readers that are more sceptical may wonder why the writer fails to back this claim up with any statistics, leaving them to suspect that although a lot of honey may now contain neonicotinoids, it's likely to be present only in minuscule amounts that are harmless to humans.

Towards the end of the article, the writer explains that there are 'many plant based alternatives to honey'. Here, they are anticipating that some consumers may feel that giving up honey is a problem, but by providing a solution to this, they are making it easier for the reader to come round to their point of view. This is an effective part of their strategy to encourage people to give up honey.

The writer concludes the article with further emotive points and a rhetorical question in order to make the reader query whether they really do need to have their 'sweet treat' of honey. By presenting it as a 'sweet treat', the writer uses language to suggest that the habit of eating honey is childish, thus subtly persuading the reader that they should be more grown up and make better ethical choices.

Even if this article does not immediately make the reader want to stop eating honey, it certainly puts doubt in their minds, and although it is clearly biased and lacking evidence at times, it is highly persuasive.

4. **Plan Bee sets out to convince consumers that their haircare products are both ethical and effective.**
   * **Evaluate whether they have been successful in their aims.**
   * **Use textual references to support your work. [20]**

Over all, Plan Bee is highly persuasive in presenting the idea that their products are ethical and effective, having said that, there are a few areas of weakness within the text.

The brand name is formed of the pun 'Plan Bee', the use of the pun makes the brand sound light-hearted and fun. The use of the word 'Plan' also suggests that the company is prepared and organised, for these reasons, it's a good name. However, when something is part of a plan b, it usually means that it's a second choice and this implication does not bring such a positive message about the products, it could make the reader wonder if there is something better, a plan a.

The text uses the two sub-headings in order to communicate its key messages. These are effective, as even if the audience does not read the entire text, it would only take a glace to absorb the main points. These two headings 'Be beautiful' and 'Be ethical' use the same play on words method already seen in the product's brand name and again, this adds to the lively effect of the writing.

It's interesting that the text places the 'Be beautiful' section first, suggesting that the writer understands that the consumer is initially attracted by what a product can do for them, and that the ethical concerns are secondary to this.

The first paragraph outlines the benefits of the haircare range by hinting at the science behind the products, with references to 'antibacterial qualities' and 'Bioactive features'. This kind of pseudo-scientific language, (which is often seen in cosmetic advertisements) can be persuasive in making the reader feel that the product is effective. On the other hand, readers that are more cynical may feel that phrases such as 'Bioactive features' are actually too vague to lend any kind of scientific weight to the range.

This first paragraph is filled with a lexis pertaining to desirable hair qualities such as 'beautiful', 'healthy' and 'shiny', all of which help to make the product sound effective.

The first paragraph uses several techniques to make the writing sound active, including the use of vocabulary such as 'harnesses' and 'lock in', as well as the use of alliteration in phrases such as 'red-heads radiant'. These techniques make the reader feel that the product itself is vibrant and therefore worth buying.

The second paragraph is used to supplement the first, as it continues to provide information on why Plan Bee haircare products are worth buying. It tells the reader that everything is 'hand crafted', suggesting they are made with care and attention, as opposed to being made in a factory. The idea of the products being 'hand crafted' taps into the modern trend that favours items which are individual rather than mass-produced.

This second paragraph also informs the reader that the honey is blended with other 'natural ingredients, such as oat milk'. This is effective as it suggests to the reader that the product, made of milk and honey, is almost good enough to eat, and therefore certainly safe to use on your hair.

Don't forget to look at as many past papers as possible. These can be found on your exam board's website.

Assessment Objective 4 - Responses

Answer to question 4 continued...

The references to milk and honey even seem to subtly allude to the Biblical land of plenty, mentioned for instance in Exodus 'a land flowing with milk and honey'. Although this is an obscure reference, for those readers that do notice it, it may imbue the products with another layer of worth.

After the two 'Be beautiful' paragraphs, the text switches focus in order to outline its ethical credentials. In the first paragraph of this section, the text states that it is 'returning to a bee-centred approach'. The idea of returning to a state of affairs that has been lost can promote feelings of nostalgia in a reader, as well as imply that this product will be produced in a less industrialised way.

The text states that the company 'curates an apiary' of hives. On the one hand, the use of the word 'curates' is effective. It makes it seem as if the beekeepers treat the bees like precious works of art and enhances the idea that they look after them carefully and treasure them. On the other hand, some readers may perceive this use of language as pretentious, as it's just not possible to treat an ever changing swarm of bees in the same way you would a collection of art made up of distinctive, individual pieces.

In the same paragraph, the writer informs the reader that the bees are foraging on 'clover, honeysuckle and lavender', here, the main message is that the bees have a pleasant environment but there is also a subtext, which informs the reader that the product is infused with the beautiful aromas of these sweet smelling flowers. So, although this section is promoting the ethical side of the products, it is also working to make the reader want to buy them.

The writer presents Plan Bee as an ethical company, and statements such as 'we contribute 20% of all profits to environmental charities' (a fact that could be checked) helps to prove to the reader that the company really is interested in being ethical as well as making money.

In the final paragraph, the word 'confidence' is used three times in order to leave the reader/consumer with this as the final message.

At certain points in the text, the writer brings in some disturbing ideas, such as the fact that some queen bees have their wings clipped, or that the bee population is struggling against 'Colony Collapse Disorder'. The writer mentions these in order to establish that Plan Bee is serious about bee welfare, however this text does not seem to want to preach to the reader. These serious elements are balanced out by using methods that make the text more light-hearted. For example, right at the end of the final paragraph, the writer uses the jaunty sounding phrase there's 'no sting at the end of this tale', in order to finish on a high note and leave the reader feeling upbeat and ready to buy the products.

Writing Skills: Assessment Objectives 5 and 6

Assessment Objective 5

This objective tests your ability to:

- Write **clearly, effectively and imaginatively.**
- Choose the **appropriate tone, style, register** and **form,** according to the **audience** and **purpose.**
- **Organise** your writing using structural and grammatical features, to supports its **coherence** and **cohesion.**

Assessment Objective 6

This objective tests your ability to:

- Use a **range of sentence structures** and **vocabulary** in order to make your writing **clear** and **effective.**
- Display **technical accuracy** in your writing, especially with regards to **spelling** and **punctuation.**

Exam tips for AO5 and AO6

- Depending upon the exam/paper, there may be a choice of writing questions; read your instructions carefully, ensure you only do what is required, and don't waste time doing more answers than you need to.
- The writing questions require you to complete an extended answer, you may find it useful to draft a plan in order to help deliver a well structured answer.
- Your plan might be in the form of bullet points, a mind-map or a list of key words/phrases.
- In general, you should use Standard English throughout your written answers.
- However, you may want to use non-standard English in order to create particular effects, for example, you may wish to use a colloquialism.
- If this is the case, place the non-standard English in inverted commas, in order to indicate that you have control over your language usage.
- Be precise when choosing vocabulary.
- Use linguistic devices to add depth and vigour to your writing.
- Ensure that you match your writing style to the audience, purpose and form specified by the question.
- You must use paragraphs in your written responses.
- Ensure that your paragraphs are linked in a fluent way.
- Use discursive markers in order to enhance the clarity of your writing.
- Textual coherence is achieved by ensuring that the ideas or information that you present are linked together in a way that is clear, logical and allows for them to develop.
- Textual cohesion is achieved by ensuring that overall, the writing makes sense by offering a clear storyline/argument/point of view.
- Always leave yourself time to read through your answer as this is a great way to identify and correct technical errors, such as spelling mistakes or missing punctuation marks.

Form

- Narrative writing comes in many forms from drabbles to epics.
  Whatever the form, **cause and effect**, where an initial event motives characters into action, forms the basis of much creative writing. Readers enjoy this form because it's exciting to see how characters respond and how plots develop.

Audience and Purpose

- Your exam question will specify your exact target audience but bear in mind that fiction is enjoyed by a **wide range of people**.
- In creative writing, your primary purpose is to **entertain** your reader.

Language

- **Figurative** and **sensory language** are key features of fiction, use them to make your writing vivid.
- Use **dialogue** in order to give voice to your characters; readers love to hear what your characters have got to say for themselves and to each other.
- When writing descriptive passages, for example, when describing a setting, focus on **key details** rather than trying to describe everything. This will ensure you maintain a good sense of pace.

Structure - Strong Openings

- Make a statement that acknowledges a universal truth to elicit immediate agreement from your reader.
- Make a provocative statement that gets your readers engaged by making them feel outraged.
- Reveal a mistake waiting to happen to get your readers on the edge of their seats.
- Start in medias res to make your readers feel they are witnessing a secret conversation.
- A flash-forward followed by an explanation will make your readers want to see the stages in the process.
- Imply there is going to be an 'us' and a 'them' to get your reader to pick a side.

Structure - Successful Developments

- A **chronological structure** will make it easy for your reader to follow events.
- Use of chapter headings gives your reader clues on what to expect.
- Periodically **referring back to a key idea** will signal its importance to your reader.
- **Alternating between description and dialogue** will give your reader variety.

Structure - Powerful Endings

- A **twist in the tale** will give your reader a shot of joy when all is revealed.
- A **circular structure** that goes back to the title will give your reader a great sense of satisfaction.
- **Withholding a final piece of information** will keep your reader guessing forever!
- An **epilogue** allows you to communicate an afterword to your reader, maybe hinting that there is another part to the story after all.

Narrative Writing

Aiming at a Young Adult audience, write the opening to a story entitled 'Dark Waters'.

Any Port Dark local could tell you that going out on the water after dark was a stupid idea; we weren't local.

My friends and I had arrived at the remote fishing village just that afternoon, and at the time, we'd noticed some colourful boats being rowed about the bay.

'Hey Kim, we'll have to try those out tomorrow,' called Sam.

I nodded but was more interested in setting up camp, a task that proved easier said than done. Missing equipment led to blame, and bitter arguments flared up. Instead of laying around a campfire, chatting and joking, everyone ended up sulking in their respective tents. Later, unable to get to sleep, those little boats floated into my consciousness. I wanted to be in one, all alone and away from everyone.

As I reached the shore, I could see they had been beached just above the high tide mark. With great stealth, I pushed one into the dark water and jumped in, suddenly feeling proud of my agility and daring.

At first I had to use the oars to punt through the shallows and then, as I got further out, I began to row, pulling against the water.

'Wish I'd never come on holiday,' I whispered fiercely to myself, still seething about comments that had been made earlier.

It felt good to be moving further and further from the shore. While lights from the village faded away, moonlight on the water grew in intensity, glittering from the tops of waves, causing sparks of light to burn around me.

Resting the oars inside the boat, I leaned over the edge and trailed my hand in the water. Moonlight clung to my hand and to the bottom of the boat.

There in the depths... dark shapes moved slowly, but seemingly with purpose. No fins or tails in evidence.

'What on earth...'

The shapes seemed to freeze and for an instant, all time was still, as they sought out and found me, my thoughts, anger and my pride. Everything was noted.

Fear made me a Titan. Grabbing the oars, I began to row, and mighty strokes cut through the water. I didn't stop and I didn't look back until I reached the shore.

Those dark shapes were to trouble me for all my days to come.

Reveal a mistake waiting to happen to get your reader's interest.

Alternating between description and dialogue will give your reader variety.

Cause and effect, the argument motivates the character to go back to the boats.

Maintaining a chronological structure provides clarity.

Visual/sensory references show a transition is happening.

The moonlight is personified to show nature has a grasp on the main character.

Use of ellipsis to create tension.

Allusion to Titans shows the reader that Kim has found some superhuman strength so they can save themselves.

Descriptive Writing

Form

- **Continuous prose** is a form often used for descriptive writing.

Audience and Purpose

- Descriptive prose is a feature of many forms of writing, so your audience could be the **general public**. However, your exam question **may specify a more particular audience**.
- Descriptive writing can be both **informative** and **entertaining**.
- Descriptive writing is a key element of fiction, authors often use it to give their readers an **insight into a character**. They also use it to **create atmosphere** when they are describing a setting.
- Descriptive writing is also essential to non-fiction, for example, a travel writer, may choose to give a **detailed description** of a location in order to evoke its particular qualities.

Language

- In descriptive writing, try to apply the '**show don't tell**' method. For example, if you are asked to describe a scorching summer's day, show the reader that it's hot by describing details such as a melting ice lolly or someone realising they've got sunburn, rather than simply telling them that it is hot.
- Using **figurative language** will allow you to create vivid imagery for your reader so that they can picture what is being described.
- **Sensory language** will enable your reader to engage directly with what is being described.
- Your will want to communicate a specific tone in your writing, use **emotive vocabulary** in order to guide your reader's emotions.
- In descriptive writing it's often useful to focus in on specific, telling details, **precisely chosen vocabulary** will help you to do this.
- Try and develop a **semantic field** within your description by repeating **key vocabulary** and using **synonyms**.

Structure

- Visualising your description using cinematic techniques will help to give your writing a structure.
- **Pan across a setting or landscape** - This will allow your to reveal key details in a **logical order** and **build up** to the most important part of the description.
- **Zooming in** - This will allow you to **establish a context** before **progressing** towards the key details that you want to describe.
- **Zooming out** - This will allow you to **create suspense** as the significance of key details is only **revealed** once the description has finished zooming out to revel the whole scene.
- **Tilting up** - Like panning, this allows you to reveal key details in a **logical order**, **building towards** the most important part of the description. While panning is good for structuring a landscape description, tilting is ideal if you are describing a person or character as you can work from head to toe or vice versa.
- In addition to the cinematic techniques, structure can be created through establishing patterns in your use of sentence structure and paragraph lengths.

Write a description entitled 'The Fortress', you may take inspiration from the following image.

The blue dawn sky is evidence that it was a clear, cold night and black ice rimes the landscape.

Low tide has exposed the stinking mud flats. This makes the stone bridge seem redundant; why not just walk across this open expanse? But on closer inspection the silky, silty surface looks quick enough to suck you under in a second. The surroundings safeguard the fortress.

The bridge is a stone tightrope; it demands that you traverse it in single file. Its cobbles are smooth, rounded and slick with ice, forcing you to test your balance with every step. The ankle high walls offer no guard, if you slip... you fall.

From the mainland, the rocks surrounding the island had looked inconsequential, innocent even. Proximity reveals that they are jagged and pitted. Ready to rip open the bottom of any boat that tries to moor against the island's shore.

The bridge passes over this rocky boundary and becomes a path that drives you straight towards the castle.

The fortress wall now looms ahead; it's 20 foot of sheer, blank granite. There is nobody visible, but there's little doubt that every approach is monitored from the numerous openings at the upper levels of the fort.

On reaching the base of the curtain wall, the path slues down and to the left, herding you into a small courtyard. In front, iron banded doors are shut hard against you. Above, dark arrow slits conceal more watchers.

If refused entry, you could try and continue on round the perimeter of the island. This would involve an act of great agility, traversing between the perpendicular wall and the razor rocks of the shoreline. At the end of this Sisyphean task, you'd find yourself right back where you'd started, having found no doors, grates, drains of culverts into the fortress.

Beyond the fortress, the lake stretches into the distance, bounded by the horizon and the hills.

This piece will be structured as if a camera is panning from left to right in order to build up to the most important details of the scene.

Sensory details about the cold help to establish an inhospitable atmosphere.

Sibilance creates a hissing quality to the writing in order to introduce a sense of menace.

Metaphor and personification enhance the idea that the bridge helps to protect the fortress.

The dangerous rocks create a feeling that the island fortress is a dangerous, hostile place.

Instead of telling the reader that the fortress is impenetrable, the description continues to show features that make it so.

The word 'herding' is chosen to show that you are being controlled by the defensive features of this island fortress.

Words such as 'demands', 'drives' and 'herding' create a semantic field to emphasise that the island fortress is in control.

Form

- The main body of a report usually takes the form of **continuous prose**.

Audience and Purpose

- A report is likely to be aimed at a **specific audience** rather than a general readership, for example, your school report is written for you and your parents.
- The purpose of a report is to **inform** the reader about a particular topic.
- You are aiming to present them with a **comprehensive assessment** of a situation so that they can make a judgement.
- You can express your own opinion and **make recommendations** but do so in a **dispassionate way**, ultimately, it is up to the reader to come to a decision.

Language

- Using a **formal register** will help to make your writing sound authoritative. This will make your reader feel confident about the information you are presenting and the recommendations you make.
- Using the **modal verbs** 'could', 'may' and 'might' help to create an **impersonal tone**. This will make your report sound measured and encourages your reader to trust that your assessment of the situation is a balanced view.
- **Avoid writing in the first person**, instead of saying 'I think...' use phrases such as 'the report has found that...'. This will help to convey the dispassionate tone that befits a report.
- Use **facts, figures and statistics** to show that the findings of your report are based on research.
- Use **discursive markers**, such as 'conversely...', or 'another consideration...'. These will enable you to present the opposing viewpoints that the report must take into consideration.

Structure

- **Begin by stating the main focus** of the report.
- Develop the main body of the report by **presenting the details** of the case.
- **Conclude with a recommendation** that is based on the evidence presented in the main body of the report.
- Use of **bullet points** could help to clarify pros and cons of the situation.

Report Writing

The drama department has won a grant, write a report for the head of drama detailing how the pupils would like the money to be spent.

This report is informed by both in depth interviews with all the GCSE Drama students, and the collated questionnaire responses from all Key Stage 3 pupils.

Previously, the Drama department has proposed that the grant would be spent upon refurbishing the existing performance space by replacing the proscenium curtains, flats and downstage curtain. While these proposals would improve the look of the drama studio, there are alternative ways of spending the money that merit serious consideration.

Firstly, this report suggests that the existing curtains and flats (which are no longer fit for purpose) are completely removed. Instead of replacing like for like, the money could then be spent on upgrading the lighting and sound system in the drama studio.

This would be done by purchasing: lights, speakers and cutting edge software to control the entire rig.

Through creative management of light and shade, a focal performance area could be created and this would supersede the need for more traditional curtains and flats.

In addition, by manipulating lighting and sound, there would be scope for creating dramatic atmospheres that are just not possible with traditional staging.

Although many pupils enjoy the performance side of Drama, some find it intimidating to the point where they rate the subject as their least favourite. An upgraded lighting and sound system could provide scope for such pupils to engage with Drama in a way that suits them. They could exercise their creativity by devising dramatic lighting schemes and soundscapes.

It is worth mentioning that the current set up, with curtains and flats, can at times facilitate poor behaviour, with pupils tugging at the curtains, and in worst case scenarios, using them as a cover for bullying. By dispensing with the existing curtains and flats it would make the drama studio a more purposeful work space, for both staff and students.

All of the GCSE Drama students commented that they have observed there is a growing movement for plays to be performed in spaces not specifically designed for theatre, but that through use of light and sound, mundane or awkward places are transformed in to something magical. If the Drama department were to take on the recommendations of this report and upgrade the light and sound systems, then it would find itself in keeping with modern trends.

The opening establishes that the report is based on a wide range of opinions and this strengthens its case.

The tone is formal.

The report openly states its proposals and maintains an impersonal tone.

The report goes on to detail the different ways in which its proposals are superior to the existing ideas.

The report clearly has its target audience in mind.

Discursive markers add clarity when new points are introduced.

The report recognises that its audience is both pupils and teachers.

Travel Writing

Form

- Travel writing can be found in many forms, including: travel guides, newspaper articles, journals and essays.

Audience and Purpose

- The audience for travel writing can range from teenage backpackers to families looking for 5* luxury; your exam question will specify an audience.
- One purpose of travel writing is to **inform** the reader of key information concerning topics such as: accommodation, attractions, cuisine and customs.
- Authors can also make their travel writing **entertaining** as they share their unique insights and observations.

Language

- Write in the **first person** to show you're sharing your personal experience.
- **Facts and figures** help readers to plan, for example, informing them about temperature and rainfall will guide them on what clothes to pack. Information about the cost of accommodation and eating out will allow them to budget.
- Use **anecdotes** to make your writing entertaining. Personal stories will enable you to share **insights** about the destination and its inhabitants.
- Use **emotive language** to convey the feelings you experienced at the location.
- Use **sensory language** to describe the environment in order to make it come alive for the reader.
- Describe key attractions using **metaphors** and **similes** to convey the new and unusual sights.
- **Avoid travel writing clichés** such as 'hidden gem' or 'off the beaten-track'.
- A **conversational register** will help make your reader warm to you and accept your view of the location, however, don't become too informal or start using slang.

Structure - Travel Writing to Inform

- **Sub - headings** help readers skim and scan through a travel guide in order to find the section they are looking for.
- **Bullet points** can add clarity and help to convey essential information.

Structure - Travel Writing to Entertain

- Travel writing is based in fact but can still be **structured with a narrative**, this will help to add tension. For example, maybe you and your friend had a race across an island using different forms of transport.
- Beginning **in medias res** with a description of a shocking or funny moment, this will grip your reader and make them want to read on.
- Establish the where, when and why of the situation **near the beginning** of your writing in order to set the scene for your reader.
- **Chronological boundaries** can also bring structure to your travel writing, for example, you might want to focus on what you can do if you only have 1 hour to spend in a location.
- Don't feel like you have to describe everything, instead, focus in on a set number of **significant moments.**
- Travel is all about new experiences, **finish your piece with an observation** about what you have learnt or how you have developed as a result of your travelling.

Travel Writing

Write an article for a broadsheet newspaper that gives details about a memorable holiday experience.

The lone and level sands stretch far away.

I am woken by a clattering noise. I feel disorientated; I can't remember where I am. I look across the aisle and see that the armed guard has fallen asleep and that his ancient assault rifle has slipped from his grasp: that was what had made the noise. Nobody seems concerned that the rifle is now gently slithering around on the floor, rocked by the motion of the bus as it speeds through the desert.

I remember now, I'm on my way to Abu Simbel, an ancient temple, deep in the Nubian Desert. The armed guard is employed by the travel operator in order to keep us tourists safe. He's pretty relaxed about his role.

It's a four hour journey from the hotel to the temple and I've managed to sleep for half that time. I spend the next two hours gazing lazily out of the window. There is nothing, nothing but pale sand for mile upon mile. Nothing… and then a bus stop, in the middle of nowhere, with an Egyptian man, curled up in his robe, asleep on the bus stop bench, and then nothing again for another hour.

At 6am the bus pulls into what looks like Mos Eisley's car park. Of course, the coach has air conditioning, but the readout next to the clock informs everyone that it's already a ferocious 39 degrees out there on this sunny August morning.

Temple Facts
- Ramesses II commissioned the Abu Simbel temples to commemorate his victory over the Hittites.
- Ramesses dedicated the smaller temple to his favourite wife, Nefertari.
- In the 1960's the temples were moved in order to save them from being submerged under the waters of Lake Nasser.

Starting to feel a bit woozy from the dragon breath heat of the outdoors, I longed to get inside the first temple, only to find that the heating had been left on since the reign of Ramesses II.

Ramesses decreed that the temple interiors should be decorated with paintings depicting his glory, so that he would be remembered from his day to this day. He got his wish, as hundreds of tourists visit the temples each and every day.

But… it's not always about great works. The most startling memory that I will take away from today is not of the temple, but of that man at the bus stop, with the lone and level sands stretching away from him in every direction. And I can't help wondering… what are his victories? Who does he love? Sometimes, when you're travelling, it's the smallest moments that leave the biggest impressions.

Begins in medias res in order to hook the reader's interest.

Use of the first person shows it is written from experience.

Established the where and why to clarify the situation for the reader.

A conversational register helps to draw the reader in.

Allusion to a 'Star Wars' location shows that this place looks unusual.

Sub-headings help the reader to find specific details.

Bullet points help to convey information.

Metaphor helps to describe the climate.

Travel is all about new experiences, finish your piece with an observation about what you have learnt or how you have developed as a result of your travelling.

Autobiographical Writing

17

Form

- Autobiographical writing can appear in many forms including: journals, sketches and diaries. Look at what form the question specifies.

Audience and Purpose

- Always check the audience specified in your exam question.
- A **shared interest** will draw in a particular audience, for example, people interested in running would be likely to enjoy the autobiography of a professional runner.
- The purpose of autobiographical writing is to **inform** readers about your attitudes, insights and opinions, as well as the events you've experienced.
- In order to make an autobiography **entertaining**, focus on key events.

Language

- You should use the **first person** in autobiographical writing.
- Use of **facts and figures** can help to convey the idea you are sharing real, specific experiences, but don't over use them otherwise your writing could start to sound mechanical.
- Using **direct speech** will allow you to communicate key conversations and also add variety to you writing.
- Using **figurative language**, such as personification and similes, will help to make your autobiographical writing dynamic and entertaining.
- Consider using **irony** in your autobiographical writing. Irony can help you to reveal your personality, as depending upon how it's used, it can convey anything from humour to a scathing attack.
- Because autobiographies allow writers and readers to connect over a shared interest, the use of **in-jokes**, **jargon** and **technical vocabulary** will help to emphasise this important and satisfying bond.

Structure

- Even though you are aiming to share real life facts and experiences, you should also try to structure them into a **narrative**.
- Focusing on **key moments and important events** (rather than trying to describe every detail) will help you to form an interesting narrative structure.
- Readers are often looking to learn something by reading about your experiences. To respond to this, structure your writing with an **opening statement** that clarifies an issue that you needed to overcome. Then proceed to **explain how you tackled the issue**. **Finish with a message to your reader** about how they can follow in your footsteps (or avoid your mistakes).
- Autobiographies often use a **chronological structure**, but you could also use **flash backs** or **flash forwards** if this helps to support the structure of the narrative you want to convey.

When revising, if there is something you don't understand, remember to write it down so that you can ask your teacher next lesson.

Autobiographical Writing

Write about a time when you overcame a fear.

Everybody is afraid of something. I'd always been afraid of looking stupid and being laughed at, but read on to see how the ugliest horse in the world helped me to overcome my fear.

Ever since I could remember, my family had owned horses. Not fancy thoroughbreds, or cute cobs, just horses. My Dad loved all horses and had rescued dozens over the years: ex polo ponies with no teeth, hunters too old to hunt, biters, kickers, every kind of broken down nag. He kept them all on our run down sheep farm.

One day, the owner of the local riding stables dropped round to see Dad.

'I've been given a useless hunter, he's glue unless you want him?' she said in her usual no-nonsense manner.

Dad had that 'useless hunter' back at the farm within the hour.

Pickles was brown. Not a glowing chestnut, or a striking bay, he was just brown, like the colour of over-cooked liver. What's more he was fat, lazy and couldn't canter properly, instead opting for an ungainly, rolling kind of run. It was no wonder he'd been given away.

'Take him out for hack, see what he's like,' said Dad.

Pickles was compliant when I tacked him up and affectionately nuzzled me as I worked round him.

Over the coming months, Pickles and I developed a great bond. I didn't mind that he was fat; it was like riding round on a great big armchair. I didn't care that he couldn't canter, I just learnt to roll with his peculiar gait.

I'd always wanted to compete in the local Point to Point competition, however, none of our previous horses had been up to the challenge, but Pickles was.

There was only one thing stopping me, if we entered, we'd be pulling up to the meet with our rusty Land Rover, while all the other competitors would be arriving in style, in shiny new 4x4s.

In the end, my desire to compete outweighed my fear of being laughed at and I signed up for the race.

Did I look elegant on Pickles? No. Did anyone laugh at me? Well, yes as it happens, I did get an imperious sneer from one over-groomed snob, but I realised that when I met that attitude, I didn't actually feel afraid. I could see it for what it was, just an opinion.

I also found that the majority of the people at that meet were my kind of people, because we were all horse mad. There was nothing to fear from them. I realised that I'd nurtured the fear of looking stupid, but when I faced it, it simple vanished into thin air.

Open with a statement that clarifies an issue that you want to overcome.

1st person is used to show it is autobiographical.

Direct speech brings variety to the writing and communicates a key event.

Figurative language helps to add depth to the detail.

Horse related vocabulary and terms help to make a strong connection with readers that have similar interests.

Focuses on key events rather than detailing every single moment.

This uses a traditional chronological structure found in much autobiographical writing.

Finishes with an insight regarding the problem introduced at the start of the piece.

Newspaper Article

18

Form

- Always start an article with a **headline** in order to catch the reader's attention.
- Use a **strapline** after the headline to give your reader a summary of the article, straplines help people decide if they want to continue reading the article.
- Use **subheadings** to highlight key elements within the article.

Audience and Purpose

- Your audience will be the **general public**, so you're aiming to capture the interest of a diverse range of people.
- Newspapers aim to **inform** the general public on current issues.
- Newspapers also have a particular ethos and will want to **influence** readers.
- Furthermore, if articles are **entertaining** this will help to sell more newspapers.
- People often skim and scan newspapers, so your job is to hook your reader and then keep them reading.

Language

- Use language techniques such as: **alliteration**, **rhyme**, **puns** or **allusions** in your headline to make it eye catching.
- Include **facts**, **figures** and **statistics** to prove that you are informing your readers with trustworthy information.
- Use **rhetorical language** to persuade your readers to agree with your take on current affairs.
- Consider the tone of your article in order to engage your reader on an **emotional** level.
- Your register should maintain **a degree of formality**, as this gives you credibility, but **also sound almost conversational** to give the impression you're talking to your reader as if they are an equal.

Structure

- Begin your article with a **concise opening paragraph** that informs the reader of the who, what, when, where and why of the story.
- **Develop** the most important details in the subsequent paragraphs. These may contain quotes from 'experts' and 'eye-witnesses' that support your point.
- Place less important aspects towards the end of the article.
- Give a **strong conclusion** at the end so the reader leaves with a clear idea of your message.

Newspaper Article

An Inspector Calls

Who watches the watchmen? Students speak out about Ofsted.

Schools can expect an Ofsted visit at least every three years, so pupils will experience several inspections during their school careers. We're used to hearing how teachers feel about Ofsted, but what do the pupils have to say about this government body?

In a recent survey of 14 to 19 year olds, those attending schools rated as 'outstanding' reported that this gave them a sense of pride, while students attending 'inadequate' schools reported a very different story.

"If you go to a bad school, it makes you feel like you're part of that failure."

This sentiment was echoed time and time again, with over 70% of students revealing that an 'inadequate' judgement against their school had damaged their personal self-esteem.

Even in schools judged to be 'good' or 'outstanding', pupils reported that an inspection can have a negative impact as it becomes apparent that the focus shifts from teaching to paperwork.

Ofsted inspectors report that they sometimes encounter hostile behaviour from pupils, including: verbal abuse, being jostled in corridors and even being pelted with food. While this is highly inappropriate, it is also indicative of the strength of feeling out there.

In light of such evidence, is it fair to argue that Ofsted 'requires improvement'? The answer is yes... and the recommendations? Do away with the pejorative grading and create a system that has less impact upon daily routines.

The headline alludes to a play commonly studied at GCSE to attract a target audience.

The strapline uses alliteration, and a rhetorical question to hook the reader.

The first paragraph tells the reader what the article is going to be about.

Using a direct quote gives the article credibility.

A blend of formal and informal language creates a register that is both serious and supportive.

A tone of sympathy is created by a focus on the pupils' emotions and well-being.

A strong conclusion leaves the reader with a clear message.

Speeches

19

Form

- Always start a speech by giving a **warm greeting** to your audience and always **finish by thanking them for listening**.
- Remember that a speech can be a **two way process** and there is the potential for your audience to respond to what you're saying. You could emulate this within your writing with comments such as 'I understand what you're saying, but…', this will help to form your writing into a speech and also allows you to incorporate a counter-argument at the same time.

Audience and Purpose

- An audience can easily be diverted by: people around them, their phones or the view out of the window. It's your job to be more **engaging and dynamic** than any distractions.
- Think about what **motivates** your audience as a group.
- Speeches can be used for numerous purposes, be sure to stick to what your exam question has asked you to do with it.

Language

- Create a **direct connection** with your audience by using **personal pronouns** such as 'we' and 'us'. Also try making comments that resonate with their concerns or interests to show you understand them.
- Use both **rhetorical and figurative language** to illustrate your points.
- Use **emotive language** in a way that leaves the audience feeling **uplifted** and **empowered** to follow your lead, don't alienate them by sounding abrasive.
- Focus on your use of alliteration, assonance, sibilance and onomatopoeia, as these **aural techniques** really come to life when spoken aloud.

Structure

- You could begin by asking your audience a **key rhetorical or provocative question**, to get them thinking straight away.
- Use punctuation and text structure to communicate **a sense of timing** in the speech, for example, a pause, demonstrated by an ellipsis, would add tension.
- Decide upon a key message and **repeat** this at intervals throughout your speech to help your audience to remember it.
- Use phrases such as 'moving on', or 'which brings me to my next point' as these will help your audience to **follow your points**.
- **Finish on a call to action** in order to leave a lasting impression upon your audience.

Speeches

How would you improve your school? You have been asked to present your ideas in the form of a speech.

Thank you for attending this meeting, and to begin, here's a question for you, what's the one thing we could do to improve our school's performance? I know teachers are busy people, so I'll get straight to the point. It's controversial, but I propose that we changes the uniform policy.

Firstly, when you were at school, most of you would have been required to wear a tie. In the present day, ties are falling out of favour, no longer sported by football pundits, nor do they bedeck the neck of the businessman. So why persist with insisting that the pupils at our school wear such a hated, archaic garment? Let's ditch the tie.

Then we move on to the next most hated piece of uniform... any ideas? Yes, the 'smart shoe'. You know, those black leather things, that start off shiny, but gradually get more muddy, scruffy and scuffed until even 'Just William' wouldn't wear them. I can guarantee that my fellow pupils would take more pride in their footwear if they were allowed to wear their beloved trainers or DMs. Let's abandon the 'smart shoe'.

Before I continue, I can see that some of you are not keen on these ideas, but just think, with these changes, you'll see an end to all those tiresome little battles that centre around uniform, freeing you up to get on with teaching.

Let's consider this, we're a school, not a factory. You're not trying to mass-produce a product; we're not for sale. So why force us into uniform packaging? Clothing is an outward expression of an internal life, and by allowing pupils to choose their own, it can provide insight, and thus help to build better working relationships. Let's renounce monotone garb.

Not convinced? Then let's be SMART about this, trial freedom of choice for just one term, take a survey, calculate attainment scores. If the school's performance hasn't improved in that time...

Well, I'll eat my hat!

This shows an understanding of the audience.

Rhetorical questions get your audience to think about the issue.

Careful use of punctuation helps to create a sense of timing that would be present in a speech.

Emotive language helps the audience to connect with your point of view.

A key phrase has been reused but adapted each time to add structure.

Finish on a call to action to motive the audience to make a change.

Reviews

20

Form

- Reviews **can appear in any form**, for example, a letter to a friend or as a newspaper article. Be sure to use the form specified by your exam question.

Audience and Purpose

- The form specified in the exam question will also give you an audience to think about, ensure you write in a way that's **appropriate for your target audience**.
- The main purpose of a review is to **inform** your audience about an experience you've had, for example, reading a book or eating at a new restaurant.
- By **sharing your opinion**, your audience can then decide if they would like to have the same experience.
- You should also aim to make your review **entertaining**, so that your reader enjoys hearing your opinion, rather than feeling like they're being lectured.
- Let your audience know that your are **an authority** on what you're reviewing so that they **trust** your opinion.

Language

- Don't make sweeping, general statements as these will leave your reader non the wiser. Instead, be **precise** in your choice of vocabulary to convey details.
- Use figurative language to make your writing engaging and entertaining.
- Use allusions and comparisons to help illustrate your opinion.
- Use facts and figures to support your opinion.
- Even if you don't like what you are reviewing, **maintain an element of civility in your register** as this will help your opinion sound fair and credible.

Structure

- You might like to begin by clarifying the **who/what/when/where/why** as these factors provide a **context** for your opinions that are to follow.
- At some point in your review, you might want to give a 'star rating'.
- A clear section of 'Pros and Cons' can add impact to your structure.
- Structure your points in order and start with the most important.
- Towards the end of your review, you could provide your reader with some 'Top Tips'.
- Finish your review with a final, summative statement.

Reviews

Imagine a new swimming pool has opened up in your local town. Write a review for your school magazine about this facility.

Come On In, The Water's Lovely!

This week saw the grand opening of the new swimming pool, located on Stone Road, just a two minute walk from the town centre.

Having been a keen swimmer since the age of five, and a member of the school's swimming team, I was excited to try out the new public swimming pool.

I attended a lane swimming session, which was well organised, with one extra wide 'Slow' lane, one 'Medium' and one 'Fast' lane. This meant that even though the session got very busy, very quickly, everyone could still swim at their own pace.

If perfecting front crawl isn't for you, there are also general swimming sessions and inflatable fun times, great for if you want to muck about with mates.

There's nothing like a long, hot shower after a good swim, unfortunately, you won't get one here! The showers are on a timer and once you've pushed the button, it dispenses about 10 seconds of lukewarm water (shudder). Plus, the shower area is: unisex, freezing cold and open-plan.

Top Tips
- Bring a £1 coin to operate the locker.
- Check online for opening times and the pool session timetable.

Pros: Large clean pool, life guards in full time attendance, value for money.

Cons: Cold showers, small changing cubicles.

Clarifying the what, when and where to provide context

Proving your credentials on why your review is credible.

Providing key details rather than describing everything about the new pool.

Keeping the audience in mind by referring to the fact that groups of friends could go together.

Top Tips and Pros/Cons sections adds clarity to the structure.

Letters

Form

- Your address should be at the very top of the page on the right hand side.
- Underneath this should be the date.
- Then the recipient's address should be underneath this but on the left hand side of your page. You can make these addresses up in your exam.
- Underneath the recipient's address, add the salutation.
- If you use the salutation 'Dear Sir or Madam' sign off with 'Yours faithfully'.
- If you name the person in the salutation, for example, 'Dear Mrs Parks', sign off with 'Yours sincerely'.
- After the salutation, go down on to the line below and indent your first line of writing.

Audience and Purpose

- Your exam question will specify an audience but it could range from someone in authority, such as a head teacher, to a friend. Ensure your register matches.
- Today, letters tend to be used in order to communicate in a formal way, often to express dissatisfaction or to pitch a strong argument.

Language

- If your letter is to someone in a position of authority, use **Standard English** and adopt a respectful tone.
- If your letter is to a peer, your language can be more conversational.
- Even if a letter is informal, do not use any text speech or abbreviations.
- If the purpose of your letter is to be persuasive, use rhetorical language to enhance your point.
- If the purpose of your letter is to express dissatisfaction, use emotive language to communicate your feelings.

Structure

- If your letter has a formal purpose, begin by stating your case, this will bring clarity to your structure.
- Work through the points you wish to make, placing them **in order of importance**.
- Use discourse markers such as 'Furthermore...' to add clarity and fluency.
- If the letter is formal, end with a paragraph stating how you wish the situation to unfold. If the letter is informal, end with a pleasantry, such as a comment about looking forward to seeing your friend or family member in the near future.

Letters

A charity is offering a free place on an arctic expedition, in order to study wildlife and climate change. Write a letter to apply for this place.

80, High Street,
Mundesley,
Norfolk,
NR11 8JL.

15th February, 2018.

Professor Eriksen,
Svalbard Trust,
52, Hilmar Rekstens Vei,
Longyearbyen,
Svalbard.

Dear Professor Eriksen,

I have had a long fascination with wildlife and would dearly love to join the expedition in order to further my understanding of how climate change is affecting the environment and its inhabitants.

My love of wildlife began when I was given a 'Book of British Birds' for my 10th birthday. Initially, I used it to identify garden birds, but soon found that I wanted to see more species, prompting me to travel further and further afield. It would be amazing to observe rare arctic species; my dream is to see a Blue-winged Teal.

I am on the Student Committee and have the role of ensuring that the school is environmentally responsible. In this role, I have worked with the Head of Catering to ensure that all the kitchen waste is recycled or composted (not a glamourous topic, but very important).

Furthermore, I have recently completed my Duke of Edinburgh Bronze Award and am currently working toward Silver. These experiences have helped make me more: resourceful, self-sufficient and creative. I think these skills would make me a useful team member.

If I were to be successful in securing the free place, I intend to keep a journal during the expedition. I would then use these notes to report back to fellow students and staff on my return to school. In this way, I could ensure that others also benefited from the placement and from the knowledge and insight I would gain over the course of the experience.

Yours sincerely,

Frank Styles.

Your address is in the top right of the page.

The date is underneath your address.

The recipient's address is on the left hand side.

Begin with a salutation. Indent your writing so it begins one line below the salutation.

Start with a clear statement about the purpose of the letter.

Use emotive language to express your feelings.

Paragraphs are used to keep points separate in order to add clarity.

Discursive markers add clarity to the structure.

Points are being introduced in order of importance.

As the letter started with a named recipient, it finishes with 'Yours sincerely,'.

Spelling

- If you struggle with spelling, look back through your written work and identify problem areas. You may need to get help from a teacher, friend or family member in order to do this. Then, use the following ideas to help you master your own particular spelling issues.
- Learn **spelling rules** that govern words you struggle with, for example, you might need to master the 'i before e, except after c' rule, along with its exceptions!
- Identify whether there is a **particular sound** that causes problems, for example, you might have a problem spelling words that contain the 'ough' sound.
- **Rehearse** your spellings using the 'look, say, cover, write, check' method.
- Devise **mnemonics** to help your remember problematic words, a common example is '**n**ever **e**at **c**ake, **e**at **s**almon **s**andwiches **a**nd **r**emain **y**oung' for the word 'necessary'
- Write spellings out in **unusual ways**, for example, get a baking tray and sprinkle a layer of sugar into the bottom, then, using your finger, trace problematic words into the sugar.
- Draw a **coloured outline** around a word in order to help you remember its 'shape', this method is particularly useful for remembering **double consonants** in the middle of words as the outline will have a distinctive flat shape as is goes by the double consonant.

Punctuation

- Ensure that you **demarcate all your sentences** with a **capital letter** at the start and either a **full stop**, **question mark** or **exclamation mark** at the end.
- Use **speech marks** to show you are reporting what someone else has said.
- Use a **colon** to tell your reader that you are about to provide them with some extra information in the form of a list.
- Use a **semi colon** to tell your reader to pay attention because although you are expressing two pieces of information, they are very closely connected.
- Use **brackets**, a **pair of commas** or a **pair of dashes** to tell your reader that the information contained within is supplementary.
- Use an **ellipsis** to leave something unsaid in order to create a dramatic effect.

Grammar

- Avoid these common grammar mistakes.
- 'alot' is incorrect, it should be two words, 'a lot' is the correct form.
- 'must of' is incorrect, it should be either 'must have' or 'must've'. This rule also applies to 'could', 'should' and 'would'.
- Only use 'fewer' if you are referring to items that can be counted, otherwise, you should use the word 'less'.
- Ensure you have subject-verb agreement. If the subject is singular, the verb must also be singular, however, if the subject is plural, the verb must be plural.